FUTURE SHOCK IS HERE, WHAT DO WE DO NOW ALVIN?

Where did democracy go?

Jack Veffer

CONTENTS

PREAMBLE

This book required a revision. It was written "pre -Trump". For those of us who care about fair and just governments that live up to their founding principles, it is a necessary add-on. Our political parties have been derailed by dishonest selfish agendas from corrupt politicians. First of all, you will find that the traditional parties of the past have, over time, deviated from their nascent principles. Most democratic countries have at least a two- or three -party system of governance, with stark choices between Left-center-right supporting a religious group, working people, small business owners, the very wealthy individuals and or the large multi-national corporations and no matter the party, each party professing "dire consequences and eternal doom if the wrong party prevails". Over time exigencies demand major or minor adjustments to a party's mission statements.

It seems quite evident that the possibilities of the future seem rooted in the decisions made in the past and it is also what guides the operating platforms of all parties. Some of these platforms may have outgrown their usefulness and some of the opponent's parties may have been spawned by the other parties' actions. So, with that in mind this revision was undertaken. Many of the original fundamental party platforms were fair and just agendas for the people. The agendas were conceived from the prevailing laws of the land and in particular its constitution, but some were not. It was the protagonist's expectation that each new party thus started, with the input for implementation by the people, using their best efforts to abide by scrupulous adherence to justice for all and the protection for the rights of all. It would establish successful stakeholder partnerships at local, national, regional and global levels for the livelihoods of all, a Just Society for all, and Fair Governance for all. The list was quite impressive. In the near future we will witness one commonwealth of nations with common goals for all the countries under its umbrella, and an agenda that treats all the countries in a just and equal manner.

1. A world free of poverty where people work in peace and partnership to deliver shared prosperity in harmony with all people's nature and background.
2. People coming from all over the world thus declare their confidence in the party of their choice and the future they want.
3. To have sustainable development goals and empowered to contribute to the process.
4. The expectation is always that the chosen political candidates are honest, skillful and in service for their people.
5. A clear concise policy blueprint outlining a commitment to sustainable livelihoods and inclusive societies.
6. The political agendas of each party were designed by people for the welfare of all people and never for the purpose of individual enrichment of individuals at the expense of all others.
7. Sustainable development goals which must be realized by all nations, worldwide, by the end of 2030
8. The possibilities of the future of man are always affected by the decisions made in the past.

JUSTICE FOR ALL (MAYBE)

We deserve the future we wind up with. That is why it is so crucial that we are informed about the agendas of our political leaders and the consequences they wrought.

HOW DO WE GET INFORMED?

Well first of all, understand the origin and purpose of each political party. What is it and who is it that the party represents? If it is a party that represents the interest of the very wealthy and you are a skilled working person who needs to work eight to ten hours a day 5 to 6 days a week to make a living wage then you must know that that party is not terribly interested in looking after your best interest. So how do you get informed? Attend political meetings, ask questions, know your candidate, get involved, read and learn who you can trust.

I've included somewhat of a handbook that explains some of what has happened in the past and what can happen in the future both historically and traditionally that you should familiarize yourself with.

THEY: WHO ARE THEY?

T HEY do not speak for the rulers of the world, nor do they speak for the interests of the poor and dispossessed. They do not speak for the average working man, the rights of women, the labour movements, government institutions, financial institutions, special interest groups, NGO's...and yet as a group they are the heart of humanity; they are the intellectuals of the world, philosophers, teachers, scientists, writers poets and artists. Not organized, nevertheless they speak in a united voice about the disparity, the disconnect and the injustices in the world. Are they being heard? Sadly, their discourse is drowned out by the clamour for attention and the immediacy of earning enough to pay the mortgage for the house we can't really afford while at the same time, we are distracted by regional wars, atrocities, natural disasters, famine and disease and these events are competing for our attention with the NFL, NHL, NBA, FIFA, The Olympics and 6 year old Johnny's first hockey game. We are never more than a second removed from the next Twitter alert. We should do well to familiarize ourselves with what these learned individuals have to say about morality, empathy and love for self and others. Do we know who rules the world's affairs? "For sure", you say, The United States of America. True, they have done this for a long time, but their influence is waning. As a nation they still have the ability to influence and change world affairs. It is by far the richest nation, while at the same time, it has the dubious distinction of being the most unequal. Among capitalist nations it sets the tone for the destiny of the G7 nations through their control of the IMF and the World Bank. It is quite alarming that even in the most democratic of countries the ruling governments do not truly represent the interests of their populations. Researchers of such things report that there is compelling evidence that *"economic elites and organized groups representing business have substantial independent impacts on U.S. government policy, while average citizens and mass-based interest groups have little or no independent influence." Martin Gilens and Benjamin I. Testing Theories of American Politics: Elites, Interest Groups, and Average Citizens, p.1.* They conclude that from the results of their studies "[it] *provide(s) substantial support for theories of Economic Elite Domination and for theories of biased pluralism, but not for theories of Majoritarian Electoral Democracy or Majoritarian Pluralism" Martin Gilens and Benjamin I. Testing Theories of American Politics: Elites, Interest Groups, and Average Citizens, pp. 574,5.*

What Majoritarian Electoral Democracy and Majoritarian Pluralism means is that it consists of a majority of the population and is therefore entitled to a certain degree of dominance in society and has the right to make decisions that affect their society. The conclusion of the authors of the above-mentioned study is that these majoritarian groups often have little or no impact on government decisions because the special interest groups exert such a great pressure on the government.

That is the total impact of majority rule. We have been reduced to believing that we matter while all the time we don't. We have yielded our relevance to the privileged few that have found ways to use them for their selfish advantage. The challenge is to find out what is deliberately being hidden from us. It is not a conspiracy theory anymore; we are beyond that. It is about finding out the truth about who is really in charge. You cannot find these facts on the Internet or Fox news or CNN. You need to know where to look and bumper sticker propaganda will not yield the answers you are looking for. Read as much as you can from the intellectual, scientific, political, philosophical and informed commentaries of people like Noam Chomsky, Jeremy Rifkin, Bertrand Russell, Naomi Klein, Fareed Zakaria, Arianna Huffington, Jean-Paul Sartre, Alvin and Heidi Toffler, Hannah Arendt, Thomas Homer Dixon, Socrates, Plato... and you might get an unbiased viewpoint of how things really work and who really exerts the greatest influence on global governments decisions. One of the primary reasons that the elite fare so well is due to the apathy of the electorate: it has a significant class correlation. Some years ago Walter Dean Burnham, professor emeritus of political science at the University of Texas at Austin, related the apathy of the electorate" (a) *crucial comparative peculiarity of the American political system; the total absence of a socialist or laborite mass party as an organized competitor in the electoral market" accounting for much of the class skewed abstention rate in voting."* Noam Chomsky, Who Rules the World, p.2

Other democracies in North America have at least a three-party system of governance with one of them being a labour party. Burnham concludes *"both direct poll evidence and common sense confirm that huge numbers of Americans are now wary of both major political parties and [are] increasingly upset about prospects in the long term. Many are convinced that a few big interests control policy. They crave effective action to reverse long-term economic decline and runaway economic inequality, but nothing on the scale required will be offered to them by either of America's money-driven major parties. This is likely only to accelerate the disintegration of the political system evident in the 2014 congressional elections."* Walter Dean Burnham, Thomas Ferguson, Why Our Politics Is

*in Worse Shape Than We Thought, www.informationclearinghouse.info/
article40546*

The decline of democracy is no less striking in the European Union as all decisions on crucial fiscal issues are deferred to Brussels, the political seat of government for the Union. The disdain for democracy was most apparent during the financial crisis in Greece when brutal austerity measures were unilaterally imposed on the country with no input permitted from the Greek parliament or the Greek citizenry. The triumvirate consisting of the IMF, the European Commission and the European Central Bank instituted draconian measures to reduce Greece's debt, which not only dismally failed but actually increased the debt with regards to GDP and caused the collapse of Greece's fabled social life.

In the face of all this uncertainty and global changes we also face the continuous threat of global nuclear war. Today the threat of a nuclear disaster is greater than ever because of the possibility of a terrorist nuclear strike anywhere in the world. The great powers, the United States and Russia, are pursuing a dangerous game of one-upmanship with a limited attack by either side that could easily escalate into an over reaction by the other side causing a full-scale nuclear Armageddon. It is not a reassuring fact that the Pentagon's proposed trillion-dollar expansion of their nuclear weapons programme is touted to act as a deterrent and even though it might be a boon for the economy, it would not lessen the risk of world war three. There are enough flashpoints around the world that might embroil the two world powers into a protracted war. This *"apocalyptic"* scenario is not a recipe for a peaceful, good nights' sleep. Yet in full recognition of all that is wrong with the world today; global warming, the threat of natural disasters, all out war, terrorism, political disparities, global upheavals… and on and on, it is inevitable that the new information age is imminent with all its' attendant prospects of a smarter, better world, and despite all the dangers we face, it is appropriate, I think, to invoke an old cliché *"damn the torpedoes, full speed ahead". From "Damn the torpedoes, full speed ahead!" a famous order issued by Admiral David Farragut during the Battle of Mobile Bay August 5, 1864.*

To re-iterate: Intellectuals are the heart and soul of a society and it seems that those that side with the ruling government are honoured and praised in their society while those that are dissident and critical of government are often labeled "corrupters of the young" and punished. It's been like that since Socrates was made to drink hemlock, as a death sentence for his anti-democratic views. Notwithstanding their views, intellectuals are privileged, and these privileges confer responsibilities to be the conscience of the society in which they live and they should be driven to deliver their pronouncements without fear of punishment. It is crucial that we familiarize ourselves with what they have to say so that we can make informed decisions based on informed rhetoric and not on the propaganda served up by the stakeholders of an ego-driven agenda.

Many people are simply not interested in finding out about the realities of life and the subsequent impact it has on their own daily lives, so they are actively seeking distractions to escape the mind-numbing dreariness. The likelihood of not succeeding in the new era is therefore great. That is why it is paramount, for our continued survival, to stay informed. Get your news from reliable sources. Don't be fooled, reality TV beckons as an opiate for boredom, so that's not the place to gather your information. Non-reality and untruth abound. Our institutions- government, judiciary, law enforcement, hospital, unions, social and regulatory agencies that, in the past, lent truth, order, stability and coherence can no longer be relied upon to provide relevant guidance for the new order. The economic and social failures of our society have left us numb with doubt and no remedy seems to be in sight. Is it any wonder that in the face of all this many people have simply given up?

There is a silver lining: The promise and possibilities of impending changes beckon. In fact, the changes that are coming are inevitable. It's not surprising that, as we contemplate the future, we see glimpses of opportunities and future wealth. Glimpses are portrayed in the superhero characters of today's comic books of DC and Marvel. These heroes demonstrate extra-ordinary powers; whether it is the speed of The Flash or the superpowers of Superman or the mental acuity of an advanced race of people from a distant civilization, it provides us with traces of what we will be like in the future. Don't laugh because it wouldn't be the first time that imagination has trumped reality. Consider space travel, robots, hover-boards, holograms and flying cars... The superpowers of our future heroes already exist or are in active development in labs, hospitals and research facilities around the world. The Higgs Boson, the God particle, has been discovered in the CERN lab with the cooperation of thousands of people around the world, its implication has not yet been determined but all the participants have an inkling of its amazing possibilities. Most of the changes will take form from outside of the established power structure. It will emanate from a place not fully expected, that is to say, from the brightest and most inventive minds humanity can produce. At the same time a growing awareness is taking shape that encourages everyone of us to become empathetic while pursuing our individual place in the new world of technology.

New ways of creating wealth don't come along very often and they usually bring with them new ways of doing things. It changes family dynamics and the way we carry out everyday life. Such a new wealth system is about to explode on the scene, brought about by a new civilization of consumers: those that shop on the Internet. Today's wealth "revolution" will not only replace old technologies, but it will also profoundly alter institutions as today's traditional role economies change into knowledge economies. This Internet generation will radically change the way we do things. It will affect the way we buy art, music, fashion, cars, food, the way we bank and the way we exercise and meditate. It will develop new attitudes in the way we practice religion and, in the way, that it will profoundly alter personal freedom. "Big brother watching" George Orwell's novel, "1984", describes a fictional character that watches the citizenry of Oceania for its own sake, is now a real and present threat. We can only imagine in how many different ways we are spied upon. We have the technology to spy on everyone in the world from 1000's of miles away.

No longer will we have to wait for consensus to build on pressing issues, the immediacy of the moment screaming for attention on the Worldwide Web. It will foist decisions upon us, which may not always be the ones we endorse. Today millions of people hate America and some wish death upon the United States and all that is therein. Most often, reasons for this intense animosity ranges from its ambitions for world domination to the perceived lack of empathy for the plight of the oppressed and dispossessed, even though the generosity of the American people is legendary.

Just as America has accumulated the greatest trade deficit in its history, it is now poised to spearhead the new way of creating wealth. At the same time this new wealth creation is threatening the old embedded political and financial interests around the globe while it is, also generating radical changes in the roles that women, racial, gay, ethnic, religious and other groups are fulfilling in the development of the information age. These emergent cultures are no longer quiet and are shedding their former images of docility and exchanging it for a more active part for their rightful place in the sun. As a consequence, billions of us are already feeling its' effect, some nations are declining under its crushing weight while, at the same time, others are rising up to experience a most astonishing emergence from obscurity. Wealth building, in the new age, will no longer be about strictly American domination, but the other trading nations throughout the world are quickly catching up and will, no doubt, surpass it in time. Just as economic and cultural roles are shifting so are academic boundaries eroding too. From elementary school to university level, more and more course material is attempting to stay relevant with a redesigned course load that is in tune with the requirements of the new commerce base.

The world is changing inexorably and forever, never to be the same again. Take for instance the spring uprising in the Arab world which has been a splendid show of courage and a commitment to the democratization of a previously Sharia ruled world. The struggle is ongoing while at the same time, in cities in the U.S., people are fighting to defend civil rights that had been won in long and bloody struggles and these are now under acute assault. Each of these events, taken separately, can be seen as moves to gain a strategic advantage in the world's most important areas. What is happening in the decayed industrial heartland in the United States is nothing less than a fight to the death for the richest prize in the world for foreign investment, a prize the U.S. intends to keep for itself and that of its allies in this new world economy. In spite of all the pending changes to eliminate our dependency on fossil fuel, the control of the energy reserves, directly or indirectly, in the Middle East will still result in the significant dominance of the world. Each of these moves as a microcosm of propensities is calculated to give significant advantages to its protagonists. If anyone thought that these plans came about by accident, they would be sadly mistaken. It was decided a long time ago, since the beginning of world war two, that the U.S. would pursue its area of domination. It was named the "Grand Area", an area including the Western Hemisphere, the Far East, and the former British Empire with its vast Middle East energy resources. The U.S. made it clear that they would maintain unquestioned authority over those areas and would ensure this through its military and economic power. A pragmatic U.S. leadership from Eisenhower on realized that Europe would probably choose a different and independent direction, a direction that was aided and abetted by the American inspired, Marshall Plan that helped facilitate the reconstruction of Europe after world war two. The Grand Area plan has required and continues to demand a huge amount of resources for the maintenance of its mighty military industrial complex. Every president since Eisenhower has re-affirmed America's right to use military force to protect its control and to maintain uninhibited access to oil supplies and other strategic resources. The fancy rhetoric used to portray Americans as the protectors of world peace could not hide the fact that they were losing control over the oil resources in Iraq and so it was decided to invade Iraq and rid the country of its weapons of mass destruction. These weapons were never found but nevertheless president Bush used the opportunity to inform congress that U.S. forces would have to remain in Iraq or run the risk of losing control of the oil resources there. This is yet one more example to demonstrate what they will go through to protect their own interests. Notwithstanding the Arab spring uprisings and the attempt for democratization of the Arab world, the United States and its Western allies are thought to do whatever they must to prevent real democracy from taking root in the Arab world and although this fact appears to be well accepted by some "insiders" it is not widely accepted in the rest of the world. This is one of the reasons why Arabs view, rightly or wrongly, the United States and its ally Israel as a continuing major threat in the area. Conversely only about 10% view Iran as a threat in the region with the majority believing that if Iran had nuclear weapons, security in the region would be possible. Obviously, these narratives are very one-sided and self serving and depending on which side you're on, you can passionately hold on to one narrow viewpoint while completely disregarding the validity of the other. In the new economy, global dominance should no longer be a talking point and in its stead, we should be able to contemplate a world that is equal, sharing and just.

Perception is still 100% of the truth. We believe what we hear and so in that vain we are served up stories that stroke our imagination. Many feel that elections, particularly American elections, are but public relations charades orchestrated by the best advertisers and marketing gurus. As a matter of fact, to prove this point President Obama received an award from the industry for the best-run campaign in 2008. Presidential candidates since Ronald Reagan are marketed like commodities and the bigger the budget the better the campaign. The 2008 election was estimated to have cost $2 billion. This funding came mostly from corporate donations. The 2016 presidential elections, it is estimated, cost twice as much. None of this is problematic for the wealthy for they are the ones who benefit since they are also the biggest campaign contributors. With big donations come big benefits. This is the way it has been for a long time. The biggest benefactors of the way big money benefits are the banks, just the fact that the banks can borrow at lower rates, thanks to a purposely built-in tax subsidy, so says Bloomberg news quoting an IMF working paper:" *taxpayers give big banks $83 billion a year, a matter that is crucial to understanding why the big banks present such a threat to the global economy. David Shipley at davidshipley@bloomberg.net.* The banks and investment firms make risky investments with virtually no risk to themselves, because of the government decision that *"Banks are too big to fail" The colloquial term "too big to fail" was popularized by U.S Congressman Stewart McKinney in a 1984 Congressional hearing, discussing the Federal Deposit Insurance Corporation's intervention with Continental Illinois. The term had previously been used occasionally in the press.*

This has been the rule since the Reagan years, when deregulation was first set in motion, each crisis more dangerous to the global economy than the previous one with no risk to the banks, for they can run to the state for the inevitable bailout, but at extreme risk to the general population and the economy. Remember 2008 when a global meltdown was narrowly averted. It is therefore evident that extreme oversight is required, oversight that banks don't want, and government is not about to enforce. This continued malfeasance needs a scapegoat, so propaganda must find others to blame in this ongoing horror story: they blame teachers, public sector workers with their huge salaries and fat pensions, the immigrants for they form a threat to the local low wage earners for the jobs that no one else wants to do. And it works for the gullible public gobbles it up; it is easier for them to vent their anger on the lowest amongst us than on the wealthiest corporations. Wealth and power are held in very few hands while at the same time real incomes for most of us has stagnated to a point where now many of us need to take on second and third jobs just to make ends meet. This must change in order to go forward in the new economy. The super rich, the one percent, are not bothered by this inequality as many are protected by the government insurance coverage aptly called "too big to fail". That policy allows the very wealthy the opportunity to take enormous risks covered by the assuredness that no matter how foolhardy the financial risks they take the government will bail them out.

THE WORLD OF TOMORROW

I n his bestselling book, *Radical Evolution,* Joel Garreau, tells us that we are on the cusp of the most radical changes in man's history. Based on the devastating turmoil a tortured humanity is going through, it's pretty clear that we have entered another stage of human evolution. The major advances in computer technology, quantum computers, artificial intelligence, mental and other social illnesses, genetic engineering, robotics, nanotechnologies and miniaturization, are altering our brain, our consciousness and our sub consciousness, our genes right down to the cell level, our very being and our off-springs' knowledge right down to the core. Within the next ten to twenty years the new information age will have taken root and morphed man's very destiny into the biggest upheaval we have ever witnessed in our short history. Instead of being surprised by it we will accept these changes and let it lead us to wherever it takes us, whether it be to the outer limits of the universe or to black holes or to heaven where there is no more illness or disease. Hopefully it will lead us to a place where we can savour the essence of our humanity, of love and empathy and everlasting peace. But first we need to understand who we are. One thing is certain, the computer age with all its convergent technologies, robotics, nanotechnology, nanobots, artificial intelligence and virtual reality will ensure that we will never be the same again. It will no longer be business as usual with the same drudgery that got us through the industrial age, but exciting exploits the extent of which we can barely fathom. We will explore some of these changes a little later on. If you think that all of this is brand spanking new you have not kept up with the latest developments in the areas of sport enhancements for example where athletes are made stronger and more enduring. They walk amongst us every day waiting for other challenges that will be able to put their enhanced status to other uses. If you've seen movies like Universal Soldier, you understand what's at stake and how misguided we can become, what with gene cloning we can potentially build a race of super humans, with superhuman strength and superhuman intelligence. Most significant scientific advances come from the need to build the best weaponry and equipment, the latest things in X-ray vision for example and a prototype suite that allows soldiers to carry 200 lbs. of equipment while at the same making it feel as if it's only 5 lbs. and allowing the soldier to jump 30 feet in the air with a single bound.

In the past all of man's technology was aimed at controlling our environment such as fire and clothing for ways to ward off the elements and developing better methods to grow our food. We looked for ways to build safer housing and safer drinking water. We also developed faster and safer ways of transportation and antibiotics to help fight infections and disease.

Now we have started to merge the new technologies with our minds and our personalities. These new technologies; the next frontier, quoting Gregory Stock, director of the Program on Medicine, Technology and Society at the UCLA School of Medicine, "are aimed at our own selves." Throughout man's history we've always improved our lot with new technological advances and inventions that benefited us in profound and significant ways, the wheel, fire, cement, irrigation systems, running water, flushing toilets, communications, the printing press, the steam engine, cars etc… but the changes in the new information age are unprecedented, exponential, convergent and are transforming human nature. It used to be fiction but it isn't any longer. We are moving ahead into uncharted waters and maybe in the future we'll all be able to say:" Beam us up Scotty". But lines that define who and what we are have become blurred. Sexual boundaries in particular are becoming the most confounding to a new generation of young people. The greatest transformation will occur in how we view our own sexuality. Sexual boundaries are no longer static, we are searching for a expanded significance in our own sexuality and traditional church definitions no longer suffice. An expanded view of parenthood, of family and social responsibilities has to be defined to fit the confines of this new age. Today some even argue that the categorization of man and woman as "he" and "she" is in itself too narrow a definition as it forces men and women into formfitting roles that fail to accurately define what role we will play in this new economy. Whereas before we were expected to develop our gender identity totally along traditional male/female rules and these rules were carefully orchestrated to fit the social mold:

1. The need for two people one male and one female to marry
2. The need for procreation to sustain our species
3. The formal roles we play to maintain family units and social requirements.

All or some of these rules are now being questioned. No longer do we view the traditional roles we play as cast in stone and think that these roles are sacrosanct. It is the very nature of the role of the sexes. The values we hold are no longer as important and the young are looking for a better definition. In the new economy the young view a shift in material roles as the recasting of their sexuality; a value that views labour in the new economy as both of material and cultural value. In this fashion they get a better feeling about the equality they now hold with their opposite.

Even though we don't think much of them today, some of the predictions way before they happened were noteworthy and demonstrated that fiction often preceded reality in an uncanny fashion: Television and mobile phones, GPS, cell phones, digital photography, the Internet, laser printers, the I-Pad, 3D printers… all these were predicted in the early to mid 1900's well before any-one could seriously contemplate these new devices as anything but fictional gadgets. There are thousands more; too many to name them all.

Some predictions in the early 1900's seemed so farfetched at the time that the predictors would sometimes be sent to jail for try-ing to "defraud" the public. One such individual was Lee De Forest who predicted that soon we would be able to transmit the human voice across the Ocean. The claim was thought to be so outrageous that prosecutors charged Lee with fraud and the only reason he made this claim was to try to swindle potential investors out of their money. He was convicted and sent to jail with a stern warning from the presiding judge that he should stop making such outlandish claims. Lee De Forest was the inventor of the radio and president of his own company, RCA. The digital and scientific knowledge base are exploding in all directions. Scientists are studying dark matter, anti-matter and anti-hydrogen. While others are studying supra-molecular chemistry, memory research, optics, nanotechnol-ogy, energy, medicine, conductive polymers and many others. The future sure looks bright, for the bright among us. The world infor-mation technology market has surpassed $10 trillion dollars a year and is served by over 1,000,000 companies worldwide and changes are occurring at such a pace that these numbers are already obsolete.

If we fast-forward to the next twenty years what will the children of then look like if we use the same predictors that got us up to this point: Well if you're like most parents in 2036 you love your children dearly. Your 15-year-old son, John, is home from university and you are so proud of him since he graduated summa cum laude. He put himself through school and he has now enrolled in a fancy law school called Harvard where he will compete with other kids his age. His best friend is SAIR19, a sentient artificial intelligence robot, named Charlie. Charlie takes care of your son's needs, personal valet, confidant, personal physician, work-out buddy and a myriad other task, too numerous to mention. You want to hear all about Johnny's accomplishments since he has not been home for several months. A parent's role in 2036 has changed even though we have the same proud love for our children we don't worry so much any more about their wellbeing since they all travel with their own sentient robots. In 2036 the children have all been enhanced with the most up to date "natural" improvements. Artificial intelligence implants are now commonplace and renders the recipient a thousand times smarter than a similar person without the AI enhancement. The kids_of 2036_are remarkable. They have astonishing thinking capacity. Johnny is much more creative and much, much faster than the kids of 2016. His deductive reasoning and his ability to conceptualize new ideas are truly amazing. Total recall and a photographic memory are standard, and he can read and understand an electronic book in seconds. He is physically perfect and aesthetically beautiful and even though he doesn't exercise much his body is remarkably fit. The young people of 2036 talk casually about their bisexuality, their life's longevity, perhaps living until they are 200 years and life thereafter, whether it is another career or life after life, it seems seamless to them.

They also seem to handle pain much better than we can in 2016. John tripped and gashed his knee. The deep open wound freaks me out and I want to rush him to the emergency department. He just looks at me and says:" Don't worry dad." Sure, enough after he stares at the open wound for a few minutes the bleeding stops, and I can see the wound starting to heal in front of my eyes. "Johnny does it not hurt?" I ask. "No dad." he answers, "don't you remember, I got vaccinated against pain?"

John and his friends now have the ability to stay in communication, not by texting any longer but through a method that is not unlike telepathy. It is silent messaging and can be used over great distances, probably ten miles or more. Everyday the distance is extended further and further. The communication is engaged by tilting the head in a certain way as if it is to engage a part of the brain. It's more like a switch, although some maintain that it is to notify about the impending communication since it takes concentration to telepathically communicate and warning is required. Telepathic communications is a bit tricky and takes some practice too learn. At first you wind up with many wrong addresses and often you'll wind up talking with a bunch of people, group talking. Now it is easier because you've practiced capturing just one account and the speed and efficiency of quantum computers is much improved.

Johnny's endurance is mind blowing both physically and mentally. He can stay awake for extended periods of time, as long as a week or more. Even after a week he still has plenty of energy and he jokes with his friends about the fact that we, the parents, need so much more sleep than they do. They compare us to sloths. Everything is changing on a daily basis to match new realities.

Such is the stuff made of the future. Now that we have an inkling of what the future has in store for us let's analyze how we get from here to there.

Just like the telegraph and the steam engine changed the world of the 18 and 1900's in ways we never dreamed of, so will the age to come, this information age, change the world of today and tomorrow in ways we can barely fathom. The industrial age was characterized by the rape and pillage of earth's riches, iron ore, coal, diamonds and oil and so on. It left the lasting legacy of greed and malfeasance that spelled the near finish of life on earth. The new age promises to become a kinder gentler world an age that will bring forth, innovation, ingenuity and empathy. Computers have reached speeds of one petaflop (A petaflop is one quadrillion operations per second. that is 1000 trillion operations.) With over 2 billion computers in use worldwide, surely, in this day, they will be used for the common weal. Faster than the growth of computers in the world is the growth of the knowledge-based industry itself. If the 3 billion cellphone users is an indication of the exponential growth in the communication industry we now see a parallel growth in the use of smart phones, these are integrated cell phones with added capabilities to seek out information, perform off-site tasks, monitor your house while you're away, control machinery, turn things on and off remotely, play games and use it in ways that are only restricted by the mind's inventiveness. In the next 20 to 30 years AI will take over the world economy, from research, to games, to computers, to robots and nanobots all will be driven with possibilities only the mind can barely conceive.

Henry Ford ripped open the earth for its prized iron ore, at one end of his newly invented assembly line process, while at the other end of the process he produced millions of shiny new model T fords, available in any colour as long as it was black. The corporations of the industrial age spawned entities that were considered individuals with lives of their very own and with allegiance to no one except its shareholders. It was an odd world indeed, made to accommodate the strangest of bedfellows only to make this a world unequal for most and yet to accommodate the inequality that left some, the privileged few, wealthy beyond their dreams. In retrospect the 20th century can only be explained as a period of bloody, perplexing and confusing, ideologies, with military and economic upheaval that toppled systems of governments and polarized political and religious doctrines into large monoliths of technocratic bureaucracies. The system forced its people to walk in mind-numbing lockstep with its masters. The new age promises to be much more liberating. I think we will go through a period of confusion first, a period where we will question many things that were at first held out to us as nothing less than the whole truth so help us God and then turned out to be nothing but smoke and mirrors. What a disappointment. But we are a resilient lot, ready to go on with wild abandon onto the next stage of existence hopeful that this time ... maybe. Somehow the age we've left behind was the most blood-soaked, dangerous period in humanities' history. In the 40's we went nuclear, if you remember. Then we engaged in a protracted cold war with our finger poised on the thermo-nuclear button for the next 50 years. The outcome of the cold war was that neither side could be declared victorious. As a consequence, it was deemed far more prudent to remove the finger from the nuclear button. We've lived in the shadow of annihilation and yet with such fragility in the world we still managed to wage war in Korea, Vietnam, Iraq, Kuwait, Afghanistan and the Bay of pigs. At the same time, we went through a cultural revolution of sex, drugs and rock and roll, aided and abetted by the "Pill", the PC and Donkey Kong. But the Cultural Revolution and Donkey Kong aside we have problems of seismic proportion that endanger our very survival as a species. They are global warming, terrorism and religious fanaticism and they threaten our daily life in fundamental ways. We must resolve them before we can go on with the rest of our lives. Why are these issues more pressing now than they were before? Because only one terrorist act involving a nuclear device, a distinct possibility, will have disastrous effects. We're all inextricably connected to each other in some profound ways and one populous religious fanatical sect of Islam for example, due to its strategic position in the world has the capacity to start a global war.

Finally, we've now come to the collective realization that the most pressing issue that faces us is global warming. If left unresolved it will change the outcome of our future in catastrophic ways. And so it is that at the crossroads of the greatest changes in our destiny we face the greatest challenges. First and foremost, we must deal with them before we can enter into the information age. To be sure we can use some of the great advances of the nascent information age, but no issue is so pressing as that of eliminating global warming and its attendant issues, eliminating, co2 pollution and changing from fossil fuels to renewable fuels. It has no longer much to do with cultural transformation but because we are now a world connected; a "global village" wired for instant global communication, it has to do with human transformation. We are at a point in our existence where we have been given telling hints about our own creation, our deep connection to each other, our humanity, our empathy and about our capacity to live in peace and harmony with our fellow human beings. What wisdom lies there in that? Certainly, the wisdom involved to do things right this time around, should be at the forefront of our actions. Things are starting to move so fast that the next twenty years of human enhancements, especially in the area of artificial intelligence and computer technology, chip implants and memory enhancements will make us all much smarter. Science fiction is becoming science reality. So, we might as well get used to the idea that life has changed, as we know it. Nothing is the same any longer. Let's tally up what jobs are gone or are disappearing quickly:

Assembly line jobs
Coal mine jobs
Mail carriers
Pharmacists
Lawyers
Drivers

Salespeople
Servers
and so on…

Our social and moral values have changed drastically. These changes are framed with horrible blowbacks and it is no longer a local or regional issue, the blowbacks are occurring around the world. These do not seem to be connected to everyday local occurrences here but when we analyze them, we realize that they are. Unemployment is way up. The middle class is virtually gone. The rich are getting richer while the rest of us are getting poorer. What do we do now?" What follows is a seminal explanation of how we got from where we are to where we will be. Read on and hold on to your seat, the future will be exciting.

Human Civilization is divided into three major waves, so says Alvin Toffler, the best-selling author of Future Shock.

Mr. Toffler defines these waves as follows:

1. The First Wave was the agricultural revolution
2. The Second Wave was the industrial revolution
3. The Third Wave, the one that is starting, is the information age.

He contends that each wave in human development evolves or will evolve into its own reality, completely distinct and separate from the previous wave as it affects societies in groundbreaking ways:

1. Social patterns are established that engulf and replace the social patterns from the previous phase.
2. Technological advances that drastically alter the living conditions of each society; for example, the introduction of fire and the invention of the wheel in the agricultural age and

the introduction of the Gutenberg printing press, steam and fossil fuel in the industrial age.
3. Societal hierarchies and social justice changes affect law and order in everyday life.

Humanity faces no less than the entire dismantlement of a previously thriving enterprise and at the same time the up building of the most astonishing, bewildering era mankind will ever know in its short history. Opportunities not yet known to us will abound. "What is happening now is nothing less than a global revolution, a quantum jump in history" (Toffler 1980, 10; 12).

Alvin Toffler in his 1980 book 'The Third Wave' said:"...the agricultural revolution... took thousands of years to play itself out. [The industrial revolution] took a mere three hundred years. Today history is even more accelerative, and it is likely that the Third Wave will sweep across history and complete itself in a few decades" (Toffler 1980, 10).

Wave changes are visible as we endure the precursor signs such as rising unemployment, massive debt and political upheaval. When a change occurs it can roll over us like a tsunami and engulf everything in its path.

SIGNS OF CHANGE

We don't like changes in our everyday life. Changes are like bad surprises, bewildering, bothersome; an inconvenience we cannot cope with very well. So how do we cope while we must go through these changes collectively? How do we deal with corruption, lies, sectarian war, global warming, flooding, violent hurricanes, decrepit infrastructure, volatile markets and the lack of money? What do we do when we see that some amongst us amass wealth beyond imagination while others live out their lives on the streets of major cities in dire poverty without shelter, food or drink? Of a need we look away and try to live in blissful ignorance as knowledge of the truth is too difficult to understand and too horrible to contemplate.

Look around you. What businesses today are thriving? You're right! Companies and government institutions that sell gambling, companies that sell alcohol and cigarettes, illegal and legal drug dealing companies and any game provider that offers an escape from the dreary aspects of a hopeless life. We do like to escape and today it's easier than ever. TV: yes, the Kardashian's problems are virtually your problems but without the burden of ownership, virtual reality computer games, your cell phone, Internet dating. All this can be had with the click of a switch or the push of a button. It lets you tune out the world as it is and substitutes a world of your own choosing, imperfect perhaps, but thankfully the problems are not your own. But it does come at a price eventually you must pay the piper. All this escapism leaves us hung over even more with the result of even more desperation and the eventual escape into your own mind. Today mental illness has reached epidemic proportions.

During the industrial revolution, the life that we knew was a lot simpler with few complicated issues. Dad went to work at the car plant, a job he had for 35 years until his retirement, all the time complaining about working conditions but happy nevertheless, for he couldn't lose his job. Now that's all gone. There is no real job security anymore. Young people joining the labour force excited with a shiny new MA in whatever, remain unemployed not able to fathom what exactly they'll be doing in their working life. Ironically, in five years, people will be working at jobs that have not yet been invented today.

The industrial age was more than job security it was a life organized around communities that were often built by the major employer in the town where it had its plants. Everyone was involved in that type of community life. Boys joined the Boy Scouts and regularly met in the school that was built by the company. Families shopped at company stores. They attended company picnics in the summer and people would receive recognition for their community efforts outside plant life all this in full view of the giant smokestacks. It was a rewarding, multi-faceted social system that involved all aspects of the human condition. It separated urban from rural life when urban life exploded in the 50's. The farmer's communities, from an era past, felt more and more isolated when their offspring opted to join the labour force in the big cities instead of working on the family farm. When the small farms could no longer sustain themselves, they were replaced by giant farm cooperatives, thereby further distancing us from the past. We all enjoyed a long period of unparalleled, sustained wealth and the middle class, the class between the rich and the poor, was born.

The industrial age lasted about three hundred years. It brought us banks, wealth, wars, weaponry that could annihilate the world many times over, law and order and the separation of church and state. This was a milestone that freed society from religious dogma and gave permission to the pursuit of selfish desires without the guilt.

The Banks were a crucial invention that facilitated the central control of money and credit and global distribution. Additionally, what made the industrial age possible were several other crucial factors: The mass distribution of goods through a vast network of sellers like company owned salespeople, wholesalers and retail outlets. Those things alone did not spawn the industrial age and it could not have been possible without the advent of a massive transportation system that included global railway systems and the steam engine and after that the building of highway systems to move the goods from factories to consumers. So the assembly lines of the world plus the efficient transportation of the products to the markets made the industrial age what it ultimately became, an unwarranted success story in unfettered consumerism, until the assembly lines ground to a halt. What happened? Why did the good times end? We were having such a good time. Quite frankly, there is not just one answer except that the rest of the world, after watching us from afar for years and years, wanted to join us and they also wanted to have a good time and all the stuff we had and a house and a car or two. So now we've come to the conclusion after some painful lessons in economics that, given the fact that some 3 billion more people want to have the same lifestyle that we have, there is not enough to go around. What we need to do now is clean up the mess we've created over the last century. It may not be so easy because at the end of the age we may not be able to pay the entropy bill. Let's analyze what we need to do:

1. We need to clean up our planet and change the way we do things.
2. Get away from our dependence on fossil fuel.
3. Set up a new model for the way we will conduct business in the new information age.

The entropy bill, by the way, is the amount of carbon dioxide produced in the usage of the single most important tool that impelled us into the industrial age, fossil fuel (oil, gas and coal). We must stop using fossil fuel and we need to clean up the atmosphere and time is not on our side.

The information age has already started, keep reading and be encouraged for good times are here again. But first we need to undo the damage from the previous age. In the next few years, while we still have time, we must devise ways to clean up our world. All our efforts must be concentrated on eliminating the CO_2 in the atmosphere and time may not be on our side. All the countries of the world, its corporations and all its citizens must collaborate. For the next while every way, no matter how inconsequential it seems, let's design methods of carbon abatement and elimination while at the same time drastically reduce the introduction of new CO_2 into the atmosphere, by designing new non-polluting cars, airplanes and new power sources like Hydrogen cells, magnesium, sun, wind power and geothermal power. If we all work together, we can nurse our world back to health.

Some, like Sociologist Daniel Bell, call the post-industrial age by the nomenclature technetronic age and it is now commonly called the information age. It will take only a few more years to mature into a full- fledged start of the new age and thereby supplanting the industrial age. Of course, there will remain traces of the age gone by such as assembly line mass production. The only difference will be that the line is fully automated by robotics with only a few people to oversee that everything runs well. The information age will bring with it new computer technology like quantum computers, Artificial intelligence, renewable energy, nanotechnology, piezo-energy sources and bio-electronics. It threatens to obsolete the traditional banking systems worldwide by replacing traditional money with stateless electronic international banking systems using bit coins and the like all without government oversight.

Families, institutions, mass media, school systems and corporations are undergoing fundamental changes.

One of the telltale signs of the changes is a marked increase in the speed of doing business. There is a frenetic speed-up in the business pace. It can be likened to a sea wave, pushed ahead by the out of sync wave of a tsunami pushing everything ahead of itself and leaving behind, disorientation, frustration, and causing increased mistakes in the decision-making process on the part of managers. They just don't know the next business step since basic business decision-making processes have been severely altered.

As the wave hits, the corporate managers are nonplussed by the changes in the marketplace and the labor market as the markets are breaking up into smaller and more varied pieces that no longer resemble the so familiar patterns they were used to. They can no longer manage with old line business solutions and are not certain how to deal with the global diversity. Globalism is replacing Nationalism as pressure is being applied through ethnic diversity around the world.

The buying public is becoming more frustrated and is demanding greater accountability and transparency of corporations. People want to understand the role the new corporation will play and what their responsibility will be in the information age, and not just for its economic performance but for its carbon footprint and its workers' welfare.

After a generation of deaths by unknown lethal elements we now demand to know the long-term effects of exposure to hazardous materials in our factories. We also want to know why corporations could bring out 182 new chemical products in the last 10 years that are used daily in our cleaning products, shampoos, detergents, fire retardant materials, and food products with no oversight, even though we know that many are toxic and some quite lethal. The result of this new scrutiny, although it is by no means all positive, is encouraging, nevertheless. Companies like Pillsbury, Dow Corning, SC Johnston, Google, Colgate and Del Monte are now paying attention to social issues as well as their fiduciary duties of profitability to the corporations they serve.

We're also noticing labour pattern shifts that are more flexible such as more part-time work, job sharing, shift splitting and flexible hours.

There will be more emphasis on leisure time and down time and decentralization of job responsibilities. Marked reduction of from-the-top-down management to be replaced by shared management.

So, we'll need to build an adaptive, flexible style to our jobs because from hereon in, change is the process that will allow future shocks to be the permanent, tolerable fixture we will all experience in our everyday lives. The speed with which these changes will occur will be breathtaking. They will become an essential force that will leave in its wake the most bewildering psychological as well as sociological shocks.

So, what is our report card to date; let's analyze shall we: It breeds strange bedfellows: A clergy that radicalizes its young people by taking the heroic Koranic messages and uses them as a machete aimed at the throat of mainstream society. A society that has grown increasingly indifferent to the plight of it's poor and dispossessed. Runaway pollution that if not stopped very soon is threatening to plunge us into a new ice age. Relentless consumerism, which is posturing as the new religion, has displaced all other religions. Sectarian conflicts that, even though they are fought far from our lands, leave deep and lasting scars on our shores. Displaced people fleeing from these conflicts wind up on our shores and become the entire world's responsibility. Through cultural ignorance, ours and theirs, they seem a threat to our way of life and cause added stress in already overcrowded urban communities. Free trade has given us access to all markets in the world but in so doing our markets have also been made available for cheaper goods and services from developing nations like China, India, Vietnam, Bangladesh...In this new global economy we simply cannot compete.

Change is nothing new in society. It has been happening for the last three centuries except that now we are caught up in a tsunami of change and if we're not careful it is poised to swallow us whole, as a society.

With the advent of the industrial revolution in the mid 17th century there have been at least two major contributors to drive the industrial revolution forward. The kick-start of the industrial revolution was greatly aided by the invention of the Gutenberg press and the second major revolution was the use of fossil fuels.

And so, it is that for more than three hundred years we've had economic prosperity. This prosperity is now coming to an end to be replaced by what, were not sure. Although it seems to have caused consternation and surprise to most, this did not happen by accident. With fossil fuel our economies moved along at a steady controlled pace, but that all came to an end when the demand for oil grew through the inclusion of the emerging nations India and

China in the demand for oil We had long before, in the 1970's, reached peak oil per capita; the amount of oil available to every man woman and child on earth. In the 70's the world population was about three billion people, since then the world population has grown to over 6 billion. Yes, it's true that we found more oil since. It's also a fact that peak oil per capita has not increased because there is only so much to go around so with the amount of people on earth doubled and the oil production virtually the same as it was in the 1970's the price of oil per barrel has increased dramatically. The demand is still climbing. So, with oil production on life support we have quickly reached the point where cheap goods, because of cheap fuel, are coming to an end.

What do we do now? We've already done many things to mitigate the impact and maximize production. Firstly, we've gone offshore to cheaper source manufacturing. It did not help the American worker. So, the American worker being out of work cannot afford to buy anything. We're using more robotics and automation. What we've accomplished at the expense of our own labour force is to manufacture stuff that is cheaper but the entropy bill, the resultant air pollution, is a price that nobody can afford to pay. So, again, what do we do now? The answer is not simple. Do we understand the real challenge? The shock in future shock is here. It is a social disease whose symptoms are not found in any medical journal and for which there is not yet a cure.

BOTS, NANOBOTS, MICROBOTS,

The technologies of the information age will take us to dizzying new heights. These technologies are so new and revolutionary that we can scarcely imagine where they will take us. It is ironic that the most imaginative attempts to predict the future has come from science fiction writers, Isaac Asimov, H.G. Wells, Arthur Clarke and Carl Sagan... Many of these writers already knew a great deal about science. While that knowledge was a contributing factor to their predictions it is also true that they were pressured to envision cures for debilitating diseases that did not previously exist. It is hard to predict in accurate detail and no matter how sound the technology, the exact final shape and size of a product, no matter how much sense it makes and given the will to do so, will eventually get it done. Science fiction has always been the stuff made of dreams and it is the dreamers who are gutsy enough to write the future. Nanotechnology, although it is a very big ambitious idea, is not how big you can build things but how small. The builders of the information age no longer think in terms of the supersize very big, but in terms of the atomic and sub-atomic level, infinitesimally small.

The question we must ask ourselves is whether we are smarter today than we were before? Theoretically, we now have the capacity to build machines smaller than a one cell organism and make materials 100 times lighter and 100 times stronger than the buildings materials we've made up to now.

The simple answer is that we are. We need to be smarter just to survive in this new world of technology and automation. It no longer is based upon" what you see is what you get" Life today is much more complicated than that. The amount of knowledge grows exponentially. What we need to know just to travel through life today makes life so much more demanding and if people that lived only a generation ago were to come back to life today, they would be thoroughly confused by the bombardment of new information coming at them. Knowledge doubles, that is all that we know, every 14 years and it is rapidly increasing.

Jeremy Rifkin, in his book *The Empathic Civilization* refers to the changes as "the Internet of Things, as he sees limitless possibilities in the added connectivity. Rifkin states that: "For the first time in history the entire human race can collaborate directly with one another, democratizing economic life." The major technological changes in digital connectivity, a myriad of renewable energy sources and smarter aspects in transportation are letting us shift away from our reliability on fossil fuels and contemplate a new world and our role in it. This then, according to Rifkin is the definitive: "Third Industrial Revolution" because, "to grasp the enormity of the economic change taking place, we need to understand the technological forces that have given rise to new economic systems throughout history.

This is no longer science fiction. People should be able to encompass a future that includes a proliferated, fully integrated, virtual reality driven reality, where everything is not only possible, but is happening in real time driven by artificial intelligence that seamlessly functions with our own intelligence. The rules that guide our actions which have sustained us since Isaac Newton proclaimed them, those of cause and effect, have become blurred. Now no longer means now since with instant communications the world has suddenly become our living room. GPS (Global Positioning System) is now as commonplace as a cafe latte at Starbucks and only a few short years ago was unknown. Self-driving cars are being introduced and will make driving a lost art in a few short years. Each signals the presence of the Third Industrial Age (The Information Age) and the demise of the second industrial age.

Today we use more computers than we are do lightbulbs, many of them are unobtrusive incidental parts to larger systems that do more than just compute. These are but a few examples that we have entered the information age. Are we ready for the new age? Can we adapt? Is there a place for me in the new economy? Must we all be involved in the information age? What is the social and economic impact of all these changes?

"Life is fast changing as we knew it.

Things are no longer the same. Jobs are gone. Our social and moral values have changed drastically. These changes are framed with horrible blowbacks and are no longer a local or regional issue, the blowbacks are occurring around the world. These do not seem to be connected to everyday local occurrences here but when we analyze them, we realize that they are. Unemployment is way up. The middle class is virtually gone. The rich are getting richer while the rest of us are getting poorer. "Alvin, what do we do now?" What follows is a seminal explanation of how we got from where we are to where we will be. Read on and hold on to your seat, the future will be exciting.

Human Civilization is divided into three major waves, so says Alvin Toffler. This confirms what we already know.

Mr. Toffler defines these waves as follows:

1. The First Wave was the agricultural revolution
2. The Second Wave was the industrial revolution
3. The Third Wave is the information age.

He contends that each wave in human development evolves or will evolve into its own reality, completely distinct and separate from the previous wave as it affects societies in groundbreaking ways:

Social patterns are established that engulf and replace the social patterns from the previous phase.
Technological advances that drastically alter the living conditions of each society; for example, the introduction of fire and the invention of the wheel in the agricultural age and the introduction of the Gutenberg printing press, steam and fossil fuel in the industrial age.

Societal hierarchies and social justice changes and affect law and order in everyday life.

Humanity faces no less than the entire dismantlement of a previously thriving enterprise and at the same time the up building of the most astonishing, bewildering era mankind will ever know in its short history. Opportunities not yet known to us will abound. "What is happening now is nothing less than a global revolution, a quantum jump in history" (Toffler 1980, 10; 12).

Alvin Toffler in his 1980 book 'The Third Wave' said:"...the agricultural revolution... took thousands of years to play itself out. [The industrial revolution] took a mere three hundred years. Today history is even more accelerative, and it is likely that the Third Wave will sweep across history and complete itself in a few decades" (Toffler 1980, 10).

Wave changes are visible as we endure the precursor signs such as rising unemployment, massive debt and political upheaval. When a change occurs, it can roll over us like a tsunami and engulf everything in its path.

WE DON'T LIKE CHANGES MUCH

As a rule, we don't like changes much in our everyday life. Changes are like bad surprises, bewildering, bothersome; an inconvenience we cannot cope with very well. So how do we cope while we must go through these changes collectively? How do we deal with corruption, lies, sectarian war, global warming, flooding, violent hurricanes, decrepit infrastructure, volatile markets and the lack of money? What do we do when we see that some amongst us amass wealth beyond imagination while others live out their lives on the streets of major cities in dire poverty without shelter, food or drink? Most of us, look away and try to live in blissful ignorance as knowledge of the truth is too difficult to understand and too horrible to contemplate.

Today we are witness to the end of the industrial age while we are, at the same time, at the beginning of a new age. These are as yet uncharted waters with an uncertain future. This new age will be very exciting and daunting. It makes our continued existence uncertain and because we don't handle uncertainty well, many of us will tend to disregard the markers that spell out the dangers.

We tend to hang on to the old, for no matter how bad things get, we know it and the comfort of knowing somehow makes it easier than to face the new unknown, which, we think, might be worse than the worst we know.

We are breaking new ground here. Old rules don't apply anymore while the new rules are not yet well understood. The emerging technologies that will stoke the economic engine of the world and take "doing commerce" to a new level, will be fraught with danger and ethical issues. You will need to study, consult, act and reflect to help resolve these issues.

1. First of all, this burning question must be answered: Who will pay the entropy bill left by the industrial age; that is to say the cleaning up of the carbon dioxide in the atmosphere? Well, no answer? We all do of course; that's the answer. So if you want a rewarding career, you should become engaged in this growth industry; a career that, at the same time, has job security and is mission critical. In simple terms, get involved in cleaning up the atmosphere. Design tools, instruments and methods for carbon dioxide abatement, carbon capture, or any other field that helps clean the atmosphere. Provide ways to reverse the global warming trend and instantly gain the eternal appreciation of humankind.

2. Another career that is sure fire and recession proof is the design and implementation of artificial intelligence, to do anything from turning things on and off to flying aircraft or driving your car without your involvement, to robots doing your laundry, cleaning your house and cooking your meals and still have time left to put your kids to bed after it's read them a bedtime story. You get the drift, right? The major area of computer advancement and any field in A.I. will be a rewarding career.

3. The third sure-fire career path choice is in the area of Nanotechnology: any field to do with developing nanotechnology will be the greatest growth industry man has seen in a long, long time. Covering areas like medicine, energy, and computer technology, new building materials and building technology development. Ideally the carbon dioxide problem in the atmosphere combined with the removal of the carbon for the making of Nano materials made from carbon tubes is an ideal way of killing two birds with one stone. Carbon abatement and the benefit of using carbon as a building block for a fledgling industry.

4. Robotics: The new information age will take advantage of using robots with artificial intelligence in manufacturing. Also, in the 21st century many of the mundane repetitive jobs that people used to do will be done by robots with artificial intelligence. Not only will these robots of the future be "smarter" than we are, they will be able to improve themselves by learning as they go. Yes, I hear you; we already have robots in manufacturing. These new robots are not merely machines, they will be made to look like we are and will feel and look every bit as "human" as we are. You don't believe me? You'll see. We'll need to deal with the question of whether these robots, smarter than we are, will replace us and render us obsolete?

5. The way the Internet is being used today for information interchange is the way the Internet will be used, in the future, for the free interchange of "Distributed intelligence". What that means is that just like the worldwide web had a life altering impact on the population of the late 20th century and the early part of the 21st century by sharing information, so will the internet have a lasting impact on the life altering aspect of the distribution of the vast knowledge dispensation of the future, such as the distribution of

artificial intelligence software and updates (the worldwide distributed artificial intelligence grid), and the strategic distribution of energy (the worldwide distributed energy grid) and as a watershed for the sharing of all data so that all information will be available and accessible for instant problem solving in all fields of research.

These events will surely, occur but we'll need champions for these causes. You may yet see some of these things take shape in your lifetime, but it is more likely that your children and your children's children may be the champions for the development of these new technologies of the future. All you need today is to have the vision that this is possible and to become the animator that will allow these changes to become a reality. Sure, they are a dream now, but they will happen. Why they won't happen sooner than later is because some organizations and corporations, with a different agenda, won't allow these changes to take place as long as there is one drop of oil or one lump of coal left in the ground. Don't be fooled by them. Education and knowledge are the keys to change.

Futurist Alvin Toffler talks about "Future Shocks" in his 1970's book of the same title while at the same time Ray Kurtzweil and Stephen Wolfram allude to the fact that the "marriage" between man and machine is fast reaching total integration. Ray projects that probably within the next 20 years (by the year 2030), a total convergence of biological intelligence with artificial intelligence will drive the information age. Computers and artificial intelligence, because of the exponential growth factor in design, technology and price-performance, will be a million times "smarter" than man's biological brain. Artificial intelligence and not so much human intelligence will do much of the "heavy lifting" in moving the new information age forward. Advances in Nanotechnology and subsequent scientific/medical, computer and building technology advances, will be at the forefront of the new global economy.

The question we must ask is whether it will it spawn a new race of superhuman beings obsoleting us, mere mortals, in the process?

New building materials made from carbon nanotubes (sub-atomic particles), may well obviate the need for conventional building materials and not only will these new materials be 1/6 the weight of steel they are also 100 times stronger than the conventional building materials used today. Much research will need to be done to address the ethical issues about their uses and the impact they might have on our collective lives. Not the least of the challenges will be to understand the consequences in giving ourselves over to smarter-than-us computer devices. We envision robots that learn and improve themselves, fulfilling a myriad of functions completely unattended and Nano-bots (sub-atomic robots) floating around in our bodies always on the lookout for diseases and delivering targeted lifesaving payloads to affected areas of the body. One major question amongst many other major questions will need to be solved. And by the way it seems this question has nothing to do with the new age that is upon us, or it may be that it has everything to do with was is occurring. How will the convergence of brain intelligence and artificial intelligence occur? We need to resolve why it is that DNA molecules in the human genome have only 3%, about 23,000 genes; much fewer than the 50,000 that was previously predicted, of useful hereditary information while the rest, about 97%, is a vast area of what is called non-coding DNA (previously it was called junk DNA). We've gained a greater understanding of the human genome since James Watson and Francis Crick discovered the structure of the DNA molecule in 1953. Since then a host of scientists embarked upon the great task of mapping the human genome by deciding to concentrate on the DNA molecule. We need to ask why it is, since our bodies have trillions of cells, give or take a few billion, and each cell carries the hereditary footprint in their DNA (deoxy ribonucleic acid), why there is so much empty space? It is of course possible that we will finally find out that the 97% of "empty space" might be the "reserved" space set aside to accommodate implanted artificial intelligence. And maybe we will also learn that the singularity, filling all that empty space in the human genome, will finally yield all the answers about our own origin. Or maybe it's all an illusion. Our biological brains so enhanced with artificial intelligence, begs the question whether we will be masters or servants to the machines we will have created.

After all that, will we be in control over our own destiny?

Can we go forward into the Information Age without the artificial intelligence transplants? Much depends on the speed with which the new age proceeds, but it is certain that at whatever speed we progress the new age has come. We see it all around us. I personally do not see that we'll be able to plug into artificial intelligence and automatically fill our genome with all that intelligence. It will come about gradually, a little at the time. It may be true that your knowledge-base and your capacity to make decisions will be vastly enhanced with A.I. it will come about, at first, by combining your biological brain capacity aided by an "outside" source of A.I. Gradually then this A.I. will become absorbed as part of your knowledge base and then become an integral part of your biological brain and eventually it will become part of the universal subconscious. It is at that time and not before that your genome will accept this A.I. as part of its own knowledge base and fill in this vast 97% area of the genome we now call non-coding DNA, it seems.

Ok, back to my original concerns about the future shocks; there are at least four and maybe more. We need to appreciate the severity of these coming shocks. Let's look at them one at the time:

Let me preface all by saying that the economy is no longer business as usual. It is in fact running on near empty what with the end-of-life cycle of fossil fuel. The global economy is limping along fueled by a dwindling and more expensive oil supply. Not only are we way past its peak but the supply cannot keep up to the demand, as the developing nations of China, Brazil, Vietnam, Bangladesh, India and others have developed an insatiable appetite for oil to fuel their burgeoning manufacturing sectors. To compound this problem, we continue to ship perishable goods by airplane to North American markets: flowers from Holland, Turkey and South America, Fruits and vegetables from Chile. Coffee shipped from Columbia and Brazil. The list goes on and on. This is just not sustainable. We must find alternative fuels and we'll have to change the way we do things and we'll have to do it quickly.

The second shock will come from what has come to be known as the entropy bill, the by-products produced from the burning of fossil fuel; carbon dioxide; it is the main cause for global warming. The global temperature has risen 1 degree in the last 30 years and is expected to rise another two degrees by the end of the century. These are conservative estimates and likely to accelerate. No matter how you look at it, 3 degrees is a huge increase in less than 100 years. To put it in the proper perspective, the previous global temperature rise was 5 degrees and that took 100,000 years. If the global temperature is allowed to rise another 4 to 5 degrees, a clear possibility, then we won't be able to fix the runaway global warming problems. It then starts to feed on itself through "positive-feedback-loops". These are cycles that amplify the severity of the problem by moving weather systems away from their stable state to an acute and severe unstable state. We can notice the warning signs in the unpredictability of changing weather patterns: more violent storms, more violent hurricanes, and devastating droughts. It can still be fixed but we must act decisively, and we must act now.

The third one is the migration of millions of people from the most impoverished and drought-stricken areas of the world to the wealthy nations of Europe and North America. Unfortunately, these people, when settled in their new homes, are not always easily integrated into the societies of their adopted country. This disenfranchisement creates alienation, discontent and the back-lash are felt throughout the world with acts of terrorism sometimes perpetrated by radicalized members of these groups.

The fourth one is the increasing disparity between the extremely rich, about 1% of the world's population (have 50% of all the world's wealth), while the extremely poor (those that subsist on less than 2 dollars a day) consist of 35% of the world's population. Not only is the disparity widening, the last financial meltdown in 2008 virtually wiped out a thriving middle class; they too are now poor. Of all high-income nations, the United States has the most unequal distribution of income. In America, the wealthiest 20% of households earn 50% of the total U.S. income, according to the Census Bureau. That is amazing. In the meantime, the very poor about 13% live on less than $1500.00 a month and the gap is widening, the poor are getting poorer and as well there are many more of them, while the very rich are getting much richer. We must fix these problems; otherwise the world will be in danger of not being able to mobilize the next stage of its existence; after all we need people with money that can buy the goods and services we produce. In order for us to move ahead into the new global economy we're, all of us, needed to participate thus consequently we'll need to fix the huge imbalance. In view of changing fortunes all should be allowed to become equal participants in the new global enterprise and this can only be established by contemplating the establishment of a worldwide commonwealth of independent nations that have not only strong economic ties one to another but also this commonwealth will need the laws necessary to keep all the nations in line and a military force to come to the defense of any member nation that comes under attack by another. Most important of all we will need wise men and women to become the just leaders of this new world order that will need to be guided by strong spiritual and moral principles."

Towards the end of this industrial age typically the businesses that are still thriving are engaged in gambling, alcohol, cigarettes, illegal and legal drug dealing companies and any game provider that offers an escape from the dreary aspects of a hopeless life. We do like to escape and today it's easier than ever. TV: yes, the Kardashian's problems are virtually your problems but without the burden of ownership, virtual reality computer games, your cell phone, Internet dating. All this can be had with the click of a switch or the push of a button. It lets you tune out the world as it is and substitutes a world of your own choosing, imperfect perhaps, but thankfully the problems are not your own. But it does come at a price eventually you must pay the piper. All this escapism leaves us hung over even more with the result of even more desperation and the eventual escape into your own mind. Today mental illness has reached epidemic proportions.

During the industrial revolution, the life that we knew was a lot simpler with few complicated issues. Dad went to work at the car plant, a job he had for 35 years until his retirement, all the time complaining about working conditions but happy neverthe-less, for he couldn't lose his job. Now that's all gone. There is no real job security anymore. Young people joining the labour force excited with a shiny new MA in whatever, remain unemployed not able to fathom what exactly they'll be doing in their working life. Ironically people will be working at jobs in five years that have not yet been invented today.

The industrial age was more than job security it was a life organized around communities that were often built by the major employer in the town where it had its plants. Everyone was involved in that type of community life. Boys joined the Boy Scouts and regularly met in the school that was built by the company. Families shopped at company stores. They attended company picnics in the summer and people would receive recognition for their com-munity efforts outside plant life all this in full view of the giant smokestacks. It was a rewarding, multi-faceted social system that involved all aspects of the human condition. It separated urban from rural life when urban life exploded in the 50's. Farming communities, from an era past, felt more and more isolated when their offspring opted to join the labour force in the big cities instead of working on the family farm. When the small farms could no longer sustain themselves, they were replaced by giant farm cooperatives, thereby further distancing us from the past even more. We all enjoyed a long period of unparalleled, sustained wealth and the middle class, the class between the rich and the poor, was born.

The industrial age lasted about three hundred years. It brought us banks, wealth, wars, weaponry that could annihilate the world many times over, law and disorder and the separation of church and state. This separation was a milestone that freed man from religious dogma and gave permission to the pursuit of selfish desires without the guilt.

The Banks were a crucial invention that facilitated the central control of money and credit and global distribution. Additionally, what made the industrial age possible were several other crucial factors: The mass distribution of goods through a vast network of sellers like company owned salespeople, wholesalers and retail outlets. Those things alone did not spawn the industrial age and it could not have been possible without the advent of a massive transportation system that included global railway systems and the steam engine and after that the building of highway systems to move the goods from factories to consumers. So, the assembly lines of the world plus the efficient transportation of the products to the markets made the industrial age what it ultimately became, an unwarranted success story and unrestrained consumerism that left us all hung over. At the end the assembly lines in our cities ground to a halt and we find ourselves in an unenviable; without a job, house and loads of debt and a bill that we may not be able to pay. We need to clean our planet, change the global model and set up a new model for the way we will conduct ourselves as in business in the new information age.

The new way has already started, keep reading and be encouraged for good times are here again. But first we need to undo the damage from the previous age. In the next few years, while we still have time, we must devise ways to clean up our world. All our efforts must be concentrated on eliminating the CO_2 in the atmosphere and time may not be on our side. Worldwide, we produced some 10 gigatons (10 billion tons) of CO_2 in 2014. All the countries of the world, its corporations and all its citizens must collaborate. For the next while every way, no matter how inconsequential it seems, let's design methods of carbon abatement and elimination while at the same time drastically reduce the introduction of new CO_2 into the atmosphere, by designing new non-polluting cars, airplanes and introducing new power sources like Hydrogen cells, magnesium, sun, wind power and geothermal power. If we all work together, we can nurse our world back to health.

OPPORTUNITIES FOR BUILDING
WEALTH IN THE NEW ECONOMY

Just like the industrial age provided opportunities to build wealth by providing a hungry consumer-oriented society with things it could use in its material pursuit for happiness, the new economy will unlock opportunities for wealth building in areas not previously thought of. We must be flexible in the recognition that no trajectory can be overlooked. New opportunities exist not only for business entrepreneurs, but also for all aspects of wealth building, whether they are cultural, social or educational. Somehow, it seemed easier back then, as we were born into that age with most of the infrastructure already built in, after all we needed to follow the example of our parents for our own career paths. It didn't require much thinking. We complained a lot about greedy management, long working hours and boredom, all the time taking the company paycheques and building a good life for our families and ourselves. It was never enough, one car turned into the need for two cars, swimming pools and a bigger house were a must. The new 75-inch colour TV was a must to watch the Dallas Cowboys beat the Miami Dolphins and so it went till the bubble burst. No one, except the business owners, really understood why, until it was all done. The new business model no longer needed made in America stuff. The North American market with its hungry consumers, some 500 million was no longer enough to satisfy the production of the future, that of purveyor of goods to the entire world, some 3 billion consumers. Overnight, it seemed, we went from a North American business to a global business where everyone could participate. The Global model meant that we, in order to have access for the sale of our goods and services around the world needed to give accommodation to our own markets to "outsiders". It didn't work out so well, at first, because the Chinese goods flooding our markets overwhelmed the North American factories and put millions of our labourers out of work. Outsourcing was the name given to the greatest outflow of jobs from North American factories to factories in China, Mexico, Bangladesh and India where cheap labour abounds. There is no way we can remain competitive in the manufacture of things. So, we have to reinvent ourselves. Retrain and get involved in the information age at whatever level you chose. There is plenty and there is a special place for you in this new world of knowledge. There is a caveat, risks are multiplying, and the future is not for the faint of heart. As we are trying to find ourselves and reserve a place at the table of opportunities, we must navigate the murky waters of inventions, some good and some potentially harmful. We'll always sell things, unfortunately the retail stores will, for the most part, be a thing of the past as on-line shopping becomes the way of future retail. Other Internet companies will model themselves after Amazon, the largest Internet retailer in the world. With Amazon, doing fulfilment shipping for a myriad of other companies you too could open up your own on-line shop while never having to inventory anything because they will take care of everything for you, if you want. All you need to worry about is to make your name known to the Internet shopper and that may be the biggest challenge in the future with millions of other companies selling the same thing you do, how will you set yourself apart from the rest? It will be difficult to imagine a new economy without the Internet. If we had a crystal ball that could tell the future what are the businesses that will thrive?

1. Nurturing our planet and all that is therein, back to health
2. The new reality: virtual reality is a sure-fire bet.
3. Robotics with sentience and with AI, built to do a variety of tasks.
4. Nanotechnology from building materials to computers, to research, to nanobots will be a panacea for anyone that wants the latest, the greatest, the smallest and the best.
5. Space travel and exploration
6. Colonization of planets
7. Space Tourism and leisure
8. The arts of all type
9. Creativity; add beauty to all things ordinary
10. The service industry; eating and drinking places
11. The professions: Doctor, lawyer, engineers, plumbers...

In the new economy, institutions are changing rapidly. In the past they lent security and order to society; school boards, unions, courts, hospitals and government. Today these same institutions are in crisis, unsure of the new role they are cast to play in the emerging economy. America's trade deficit is at an all time high while we are trillions of dollars in debt. Do China, Russia and Germany, America's largest debt holders, risk triggering a global recession by calling America's debt or do we stay the course under the pretence that this crisis will go away? Europe, in a self-congratulating pragmatic mood for the continuing expansion of the

European Union, successfully forged a blueprint, with its 500 million consumers, and voila, a new self-contained market for its own goods and services with free access and no duties and taxes. It is all very much a work in progress. It can't all wait until everything is right, it must stumble along, mistakes and all, until finally a perfect union emerges. We are in a bit of trouble in North America, although we could model ourselves after the E.U. naming it the North American Union, N.A.U. made up of Canada, Mexico and the United States perhaps also including Central American countries. Facilitating such a union would have a positive impact on the North American economy. We too would have in excess of 500 million consumers for the goods and services we produce. A properly managed N.A.U. economy would yield a much greater revenue stream particularly because the fossil fuel supply is on life support and will make the goods we now bring in from China, India, Chile, Bangladesh much more expensive. We must realize that even though goods from China can be made significantly cheaper over there the extra transportation cost will, eventually, severely impact on the trade deals we now have in place with our international trading partners. Within the N.A.U. infrastructure we would be able to better manage our economy with less cost and with much greater care. In the new economy we'll have to give up certain things in our lifestyle which we now consider our inalienable right, for example: The ownership of your own house may no longer be a practical or cost-effective idea even though ownership seems to be a birthright built into our psyche.

Of course, we do not know the future, for a certainty, all that we know is that something life-altering is about to happen in this pending information age and against the backdrop of confusion, denial, lies, ignorance and passive acceptance it will, for a while overwhelm us. The younger generation will be able to accept the changes in stride.

SOME SURE-FIRE CAREER PATHS OF
THE INFORMATION AGE

S ome like Sociologist Daniel Bell call the post-industrial age by
the nomenclature technetronic age and it is now commonly
called the information age. It will take only a few more years to
mature into a full- fledged start of the new age and thereby supplanting the industrial age. Of course, there will remain traces
of the age gone by such as assembly line mass production. The
only difference will be that the line is fully automated by robotics with only a few people to oversee that everything runs well.
The information age will bring with it new computer technology
like quantum computers, Artificial intelligence, renewable energy,
nanotechnology, piezo-energy sources and bio-electronics. It
threatens to obsolete the traditional banking systems worldwide by
replacing traditional money with stateless electronic international
banking systems using bit coins and the like all without government oversight.

Families, institutions, mass media, school systems and corporations are undergoing fundamental changes.

The information age and the world-wide-web are causing a dizzying speed-up in the way business is conducted, while at the same time causing phenomenal consternation to occur on the part of corporate and line managers. Confusion reigns supreme as a frustrated buying public is trying to cope with it all. While the information age takes root, it is definitely not "business as usual" and as painful as the changes are, we will all need to muddle through as best we can; after all we're a pretty resilient lot.

As a result, we will adapt to a new code of behavior that is no longer tied to a 9 to 5 schedule. Time in work schedules will be more flexible and part-time and flextime will be the norm. Free time and leisure time will gain much more emphasis in the new economy.

Food consumption based on the standard "three squares meals "will also change to an "eating when you can" model. Family life will suffer to an ad-hoc model.

As globalization is becoming fact, nation states are undergoing vast changes. Some say that the predatory market forces of a global economy will make it impossible for benevolent, democratic governments to protect their citizens from the vulture practices of states beyond its borders. Others argue that globalization is actually creating, not predatory, but benign market forces that will prevent the rape and pillage mentality the first group is predicting.

It begs a number of questions to which the answers are elusive: Do omnipotent global market forces mean the emasculation of nation state politicians? Have governments become weaker and less relevant than before the demise of the industrial age? Is globalization the enemy of nation states? Does a global economy impede the autonomy of nation states? Do national borders impede cross border transactions? Globalization is a worldwide experiment into the unknown. One of its weaknesses is the cost of transportation of goods, as fuel is becoming more expensive and scarcer. The other is the mismanagement of arable land like the production of fruits and vegetables in Chile, Mexico and California. Droughts in these areas are producing dustbowls the likes we have never before experienced. All the potable water is used up for the growing of fruits and vegetables. As people grow thirsty, all out war over this precious resource is looming. A lot will need to change for the new information age to work and just like pollution and global warming is a worldwide challenge, so are the growing problems of a workable global economy.

HOW DO WE GET FROM HERE TO THERE?

W e need to become more flexible in our adaptation to change because from hereon in, change is the process that will allow future shocks to be a permanent fixture in everyday life. The speed with which these changes are occurring is breathtaking. They have become an essential force that leaves in its wake the most bewildering psychological as well as sociological shocks. The use of shocks to effect change is not new and change is nothing new in society. It has been happening for the last three centuries except that now we are caught up in a tsunami of change and if we're not careful it is poised to swallow us whole, as a society.

With the advent of the industrial revolution in the mid 17th century there have been at least two major contributors to drive the industrial revolution forward. The kick-start of the industrial revolution was greatly aided by the invention of the Gutenberg press and the second major revolution was the use of fossil fuels; coal, gas and oil.

And so, it is that for more than three hundred years we've had economic prosperity. This prosperity is now coming to and end to be replaced by an information-based economy that will rely almost totally on computer technology to drive it forward. Although the end of the industrial revolution has caused consternation and surprise to many, it did not happen by accident. With the use of fossil fuel our economies moved along at a steady controlled pace. We could sustain the growth up until several things happened that caused its demise. The first thing was the outsourcing of the production of many goods from North American and European manufacturing to the two most populous emerging nations around 1980, China and India. All came to an end when the demand for oil grew in the 80's and the 90's. We had long before, in the 1970's, reached peak oil per capita; the amount of oil available to every man woman and child on earth. In the 70's the world population was about three billion people, since then the world population has grown to over 6 billion. Yes, it's true that we found more oil since. It's also a fact that peak oil per capita has not increased because there is only so much to go around so with the amount of people on earth doubled and the oil production virtually the same as it was in the 1970's the price of oil per barrel has increased dramatically. The demand is still climbing. With oil production on life support we have quickly reached the point where cheap goods, because of cheap fuel, are coming to an end.

We've already done many things to mitigate the impact and maximize production. Firstly, we've gone offshore to cheaper source manufacturing. It did not help the American worker. - 1 -So, the American worker being out of work cannot afford to buy anything. We're using more robotics and automation. What we've accomplished at the expense of our own labour force is to manufacture stuff that is cheaper but the entropy bill, the resultant air pollution, is a price that nobody can afford to pay. What do we do now? The answer is not simple. Do we understand the real problem? The shock in future shock is here. *"It is a social disease whose symptoms are not found in any medical journal and for which there is no cure." Alvin Toffler, Future Shock pg. 18*

We need to fast forward to the end of the 21st century and imagine what it will be like. By the end of 2100 the world population will exceed 11 billion people, adding almost 5 billion to the present population. This will profoundly transform mankind on several levels, restructuring its inner life as well as the conditions in which we live.

It will result in a new culture comprising all of humanity into one human family, no matter where we live in the world. To feed so many people we will have to change agriculture; a new agriculture with one distinguishing feature; a vastly reduced ecological footprint.

What is an alarming fact today is that our ecological footprint exceeds the earth's carrying capacity by some 60%? This means that right now we are using 60% more of our resources than the earth can produce. While we can carry on like this for a while, we are using up the earth's precious capital. The earth's capital is the total amount the earth has produced up until now, so if we are spending the capital … let me explain it with an example: Lets say that you own a forest with ten thousand trees in it, and every year the forest produces an extra one hundred trees, this means that you can comfortably cut down one hundred trees and continue to do this in perpetuity and never use up the original forest. That is smart, but now your business has grown, and you face a shortage. You find that one hundred trees no longer fills your business needs, so you start cutting down two hundred trees. That is not smart because in another few years you'll find yourself with no trees left in your forest. That is exactly what we're doing right now. If we continue like this we will, by the year 2100, exceed earth's capacity many times over, without any capital left. The present model is just not sustainable. But that is not the worst of it because many other nations besides Canada, the United States, Japan, South Korea and the European Union have now discovered that they too can be consumers like us and are in fact seeking a place for themselves at the banquet table of consumer excess with the inevitable result that our ecological foot print is deepening and soon we'll pass the place of no return. The experts all agree that the 21st century will be a century of profound change filled with news of disasters.

In order to survive we will all, collectively, have to drastically change our ways. What do we need to change? In one word: Everything. First and foremost we need to eliminate the extremes of extreme wealth and extreme poverty and why we must do this, in a collective manner is because, right now, our entire system of the way we do things is guided by this one principle: Less than 1% of the world's population is in control of the affairs of the entire world. They are the 1% of the world's population who are the wealthiest. They control our values, our communities, our hearts, our minds, our economies, our work, our institutions and so we need to collectively institute a new world system of governance that is equitable, fair, just and all inclusive.

It is a certainty that changes will be forced on us and that a new and better world will emerge, but it won't come about without the complete break down of the old-world order. The major shocks that will rock this world will be economic ones, such as famine, water, food and other resource shortages. Wars will be fought on all fronts and natural disasters, earthquakes, major storms and pan world plagues will cause many of us to perish. At the same time, imperceptibly at first, positive changes will occur. We will all of us, children, youth and adults, of a necessity, need to become more empathetic, caring and loving human beings and in order to carry forward this new civilization our institutions will also need to change to meet the needs of all of humanity, the rich, the poor, the sick and the dispossessed no matter where we live in the world. We will have to feed all equally while also facing the challenge of drastically reducing our ecological footprint. This will have the greatest impact on the wealthy nations. At this moment, around the year 2017, the wealthiest nations on earth, Canada, The United States, The European Union, about 35% of the world's population consume about 85% of the total world's resources while the earth's population pushes up against 7 billion. In addition, China and India are the biggest emerging nations with about 3 billion people and they too now have the financial resources to consume like the wealthiest nations. If we do the math, based on our present resources, we can readily see that the earth can no longer suffice, at the same level, the needs of some 5 billion people. The model used before demonstrated that we consumed 160% of what the biosphere could produce. This means that the extra 60% is derived from using up the original "capital": cutting down most or all the trees in our original rain forests with the result that we will generate catastrophic events in its aftermath.

1. Loss of habitat for the millions of species that live there
2. Severe climate change
3. Dangerous green house gases are no longer absorbed by the rain forests.
4. Oxygen is no longer generated in the rain forests, the major generating producer for the air we breathe.

With all that going on and unable to get hopeful, satisfying answers about their future from factory management, unions and government, the North American and European workers are disillusioned, mentally drained and unable to make their own decisions that might save them and their families.

The inescapable question is whether or not we can survive the future world? Education is key. We need to gain a thorough understanding of the predicament we're in and then through consultation we'll need to apply the world saving remedies. To do so will require a united will to change the way we do things now. We will be forced, through circumstances beyond our control, to transform our institutions, into institutions that care for all peoples and creatures equally, no matter where they live in the world. This means that the poorest among us, whether they live in the Favellas of Brazil, the slums of Bangladesh or the inner city slums in the United States, they will have to be cared for in the same way as the wealthiest people living in luxury in gated communities anywhere in the world. It is the next inevitable stage in a world that has reached its full maturity except that some of us are still children while others are still bullies. We need to put aside our competitive nature and self-interest and shift into an attitude of collective interest to repair an ailing world for the survival of its entire people. It will mean sharing in a spirit of sacrifice what we have and make do with a lot less than we have today. The good news is, according to experts in the field, that we can do this and, anyways, that the alternative is too horrific to contemplate.

Every hesitant step we take in the new economy that embraces the equal good for all people is, as well, a step in the right direction and a step into the unknown. We are breaking new ground here. The old rules don't apply anymore while the new rules are not yet well understood. The emerging technologies that will stoke the economic engine of the world and take "doing commerce" to a new level, will be fraught with moral and ethical issues. We will need to study, consult, act and reflect to help resolve these issues.

In the 21st century many of the mundane repetitive jobs that people used to do will be done by robots with artificial intelligence. Not only will these robots of the future be "smarter" than we are, they will be able to improve themselves by learning as they go. Yes, I hear you; we already have robots in manufacturing. These new robots are not merely machines, they will be made to look like we are and will feel and look every bit as "human" as we are. You don't believe me? You'll see.

The way the Internet is being used today for information interchange is the way the Internet will be used, in the future, for the free interchange of "Distributed intelligence". What that means is that just like the worldwide web had a life altering impact on the population of the late 20th century and the early part of the 21st century by sharing information, so will the internet have a lasting impact on the life altering aspect of the distribution of the vast knowledge dispensation of the future, such as the distribution of artificial intelligence software and updates (the worldwide distributed artificial intelligence grid), and the strategic distribution of energy (the worldwide distributed energy grid) as a watershed for the sharing of all data so that all information will be available and accessible for instant problem solving in all fields of research.

These events will surely, occur but we'll need champions for these causes. You may yet see some of these things take shape in your lifetime, but it is more likely that your children and your children's children may be the champions for the development of the new technologies of the future. All you need today is to have the vision that this is possible and to become the animator that will allow these changes to become a reality. Sure, they are a dream now, but they will happen. Why they won't happen sooner than later is because some organizations and corporations, with a different agenda, won't allow these changes to take place as long as there is one drop of oil or one lump of coal left in the ground. Don't be fooled by them. Education and knowledge are the keys to change.

The future will be an exciting one, but it will also be a very bumpy with at least four major shocks on the horizon. These shocks are quickly reaching critical mass.

Some futurists like Ray Kurtzweil and Stephen Wolfram et al, allude to the fact that the "marriage" between man and machine is fast reaching critical mass. Let me explain what I think is meant by that: It is said that probably within the next 20 years (by the year 2030), a total convergence of biological intelligence with artificial intelligence will drive the information age. Computers and artificial intelligence, because of the exponential growth factor in design, technology and price-performance, will be a million times "smarter" than man's biological brain. Therefore, artificial intelligence and not so much human intelligence will do much of the "heavy lifting" in moving the new information age forward. Advances in Nanotechnology and subsequent scientific/medical, computer and building technology advances, will be at the forefront of the new global economy. The new building materials called carbon nanotubes (sub-atomic particles), may well obviate the need for conventional building materials and not only will these materials be 1/6 the weight of steel they are also 100 times stronger than the conventional building materials used today. If this is so, much research needs to be done to address the ethical issues about their uses and the impact they might have on our collective lives. Not the least, we need to understand the consequences in giving ourselves over to smarter-than-us computer devices. We envision robots that learn and improve themselves, fulfilling a myriad of functions completely unattended and Nanobots (sub-atomic robots) floating around in our bodies always on the lookout for diseases and delivering targeted lifesaving payloads to affected areas of the body.

The technological shifts invading our life do so almost without our awareness of them. Oblivious because of our preoccupation with everyday life like updating the software on our latest gadgets or complaining about the speed of the internet or playing the latest "Candy Crush" game, we don't see how these things alter the relationship we have with the emerging technologies. Ray Kurzweil muses: *"At some point, we'll be literally a hybrid of biological and non-biological thinking, but it's a gradual transition." -The future of Human Evolution and Space- Singularity University July 28, 2016*

It won't happen overnight he predicts, but slowly bit-by-bit we'll use more and more technology by incorporating it rather than replacing the parts that make us human.

In the process the greatest fear that people have is that eventually we'll lose control of our mind and body and that we'll eventually lose our humanity.

"I don't want to give that up. I'm not talking about giving things up," *Kurzweil says. "I'm talking about enhancing our experience and our bodies and our brains." -The future of Human Evolution and Space- Singularity University, July 28, 2016*

When do we stop being "us"? What with all the technological enhancements when do we become something or someone different? There is no clear delineation and we morph into a new self incrementally. It will still be us. There is plenty of precedent in our daily life now. We see that daily, as we grow older, we gain more knowledge and experience that enhances our capacity. So it is that we welcome our greater knowledge and we don't bemoan the fact that we change. Most people don't go through life without learning something. Learning is automatic, the only difference between now and the future is that in the future we will learn at a much faster pace. It should not scare us so long as we are part of the dialogue that lets us be the decision makers of how technology will play a greater role in life and so long as we remain in charge.

As we become smarter, we will also live longer. As the new technology advances, it will start to tackle age related diseases that shorten our life. These age-related diseases will be eliminated and, annually, we will ad years to our life: *"We will get to a point where our longevity, our remaining life expectancy is moving on away from us. The sands of time will run in rather than run out, …eventually [letting us] live as long as we want.," Kurzweil says. The science of immortality-Singularity University, July 22, 2016*

When will these changes happen? Biology is key too many of the diseases that invade the body and those that shorten life, for the same token we must look to biology for the repair of the body. The experts agree that in the next decade this kind of research will quicken especially due to advances in the burgeoning nanotechnology. The science of nanotechnology will permit us to exceed the limitations imposed on biology by utilizing nanobots in the body to fight anything from cancers to any other agents of disease. It may seem like fiction today but as science and technology converge, fiction will become fact and a whole new era for health and wellbeing will unfold. Nanobots will even play a key role in performing microsurgery.

"What is now a trickle of clinical applications will be a flood in 10 years, when these technologies are again 1,000 times more powerful. They will be 1,000,000 times more powerful than they are today in 20 years," so says Ray Kurzweil. Featured, Future, Singularity, July17, 2016

{Today} "The World Depends on Technology No One Understands". - Feature, Future, Singularity-Aaron Frank, July 17,2016

It is fairly certain that we will be building computers and systems so advanced that we cannot grasp their power in its entirety today. And when it comes to Artificial Intelligence (AI), Virtual Technology (VT), Quantum Computers, Robots, Nano technology and Implanted Intelligence these will be the driving force in the new age of information technology even though not much is known about them today. In the meantime, we need to ask ourselves whether the systems of today are getting too complex. We now have systems that, as part of their self-improvement, have the capability to build their own algorithms. Really? Is that good? Should we not worry that these systems could one day behave in ways that are detrimental and dangerous to the public good?

It becomes quite evident that we will need much oversight over these new systems particularly when it comes to quantum computers, AI. and implanted intelligence (II) (computers that are linked directly into the brain). This II will render us many times smarter and we face the frightening possibility that these machines might be controlling us in the future.

Ok, back to my original concerns about the future shocks; there are at least three and maybe more. We need to appreciate the severity of these coming shocks. Let's look at them one at the time.

1. The present economy is no longer business as usual. It is in fact running on near empty what with the end-of-life cycle of fossil fuel. The global economy is limping along fueled by a dwindling and more expensive oil supply. Not only are we way past its peak but the supply cannot keep up to the demand, as the developing nations of China, Brazil, Vietnam, Bangladesh, India and others have developed an insatiable appetite for oil to fuel their burgeoning manufacturing sectors. To compound this problem, we continue to ship perishable goods by airplane to North American markets: flowers from Holland, Turkey and South America, Fruits and vegetables from Chile. Coffee shipped from Columbia and Brazil. The list goes on and on. This is just not sustainable. We must find alternative fuels and we'll have to change the way we do things and we'll have to do it quickly.

2. The second shock will come from what has come to be known as the entropy bill, the by-products produced from the burning of fossil fuel; carbon dioxide; it is the main cause for global warming. The global temperature has risen 1 degree in the last 30 years and is expected to rise another two degrees by the end of the century. These are conservative estimates and likely to accelerate. No matter how you look at it, 3 degrees is a huge increase in less than 100 years. To put it the proper perspective, the previous global temperature rise was 5 degrees and that took

100,000 years. If the global temperature is allowed to rise another 4 to 5 degrees, a clear possibility, then we won't be able to fix the runaway global warming problems. It then starts to feed on itself through "positive-feedback-loops". These are cycles that amplify the severity of the problem by moving weather systems away from their stable state to an acute and severe unstable state. We can notice the warning signs in the unpredictability of changing weather patterns: more violent storms, more violent hurricanes, and devastating droughts. It can still be fixed but we must act decisively and we must act now.

3. The third one is the migration of millions of people from the embattled and from the most impoverished and drought-stricken areas of the world to the wealthy nations of Europe and North America. Unfortunately, these displaced people, when settled in their new homes, are not allowed to integrate in the societies of their adopted country. This disenfranchisement creates alienation, discontent and the backlash are felt throughout the world with acts of terrorism sometimes perpetrated by members of these groups.

4. The fourth one is the increasing disparity between the extremely rich, about 1% of the world's population have 50% of all the world's wealth, while the extremely poor, those that subsist on less than 2 dollars a day, consists of 50% of the world's population. Not only is the disparity widening, but the last financial meltdown in 2008 virtually wiped the thriving middle class; these are now the new poor. Of all the high-income nations, the United States has the most unequal distribution of income. In America, the wealthiest 20 percent of households earn 50 percent of the total U.S. income, according to the Census Bureau. That is amazing. In the meantime, the very poor, about 13%, live on less than $1500.00 a month, and the gap is widening, the

poor are getting poorer and as well there are many more of them, while, at the same time, the very rich are getting much richer. We must fix these problems; otherwise the world will be in danger of not being able to mobilize the next stage of its existence; after all we need people with money that can buy the goods and services we produce. In order for us to move ahead into the new global economy where all of us are able to participate, we will need to fix these huge disparities. All should be allowed to be participants in the new global enterprise and this can only be established by contemplating the establishment of a worldwide common-wealth of independent nations that have not only strong economic ties one to another, but also this commonwealth will need just laws to keep all the nations in line with a military force at the ready, to come to the aid of any member nation that comes under attack by another. Most important of all we will need wise men and women to become the just leaders of this new world order who will be guided by strong spiritual and moral principles."

WHY IS ENHANCED INTELLIGENCE
IMPORTANT TO US?

B ecause man's search for knowledge speaks of a universe that expanded from "The Initial Singularity", a point of infinite density from which the big bang occurred, to an unending vastness of unfamiliar objects scarcely dreamed of just a century ago. So it is that our search has not been limited to looking for answers in the sciences alone, but also involves searching in the realm of the divine. The debate continues over who or what is responsible for the origin of the universe, although science and religion are integral parts of the world of existence and each have played distinct and important roles in piecing together parts of the mystery of the universe the jury is still out and we are compelled, therefore, to continue the search. It's getting so much more complicated that we need increased brain capacity to solve the mysteries of the final frontier.

We humans have always been a curious lot with an insatiable curiosity. Since we got up off our knuckles, we've been curious.

Finally, we need the capacity to explore our last frontier; that of time and space, not external space but internal space that of the single cell. We can't get there without help, lots of help. We must, therefore, be infinitely smarter so that we can do the billions of calculations required to figure out the perfection of the single and to ultimately synthesize the single cell. This won't be possible without the aid of enhanced brain capacity through computer technology. What we need, first and foremost, is the most sophisticated algorithm ever discovered by man. It will have to satisfy all the conditions we can think of but also those we can't fathom such as: the mystery of Schrodinger's cat in the box (the cat is both dead and alive in the box) and instantaneous communications between two entities across a couple of inches distance or a million light-years away. These are the simpler ones by the way. A question we will need to answer is the mystery of our cells that come into being do so with all the knowledge built in. We will have to solve the mystery of our cells that come into being with all their knowledge built in and with the unique capacity of the billions of the cells to instantly come to the aid of one another if only one of them comes under attack. All of the knowledge known to us plus instantaneous updates is incorporated in each individual cell. Each cell also contains all the knowledge yet to be discovered and that might be the most challenging thing to synthesize for it is more than the potentiality that needs to be built in but also the symbiotic condition that must preexist; in other words, for our cells, it is never an "Aha" moment. It is therefore that enhanced brain intelligence is the ingredient that will allow us to explore time and space from a different vantage point. In order to contemplate time and space, a dimension we scarcely know anything about, we may have to unlearn certain things, one of those things is our comprehension of what time is. Time only has meaning in the reality we presently exist. In the next existence, time and space both cease to function and everything happens at simultaneously. We can't quite explain how that happens, even though we embrace it at the metaphysical level. When we die here, in this life, our physical body dies, and yet we are assured that the soul continues on a new existence, now independent from the physical body.

TECHNOLOGY, COMPUTERIZATION
AND VIRTUAL SCIENCES

Today it is estimated that there are about 1 billion computers worldwide, while at the same time there are some 500 billion computer chips, many with more than 100 million transistors on them. This is certainly not the end of the computer proliferation.

The Japanese built a computer capable of performing 4 trillion calculations per second, they called it the earth simulator and it was designed to help forecast global climate changes. While it was thought that the technology had reached its upper limits, many computer scientists agree that the new computers of tomorrow will reach petaflop speeds (a thousand trillion operations per second). Meanwhile Internet users worldwide are estimated to top 1.5 billion. Cell phone users worldwide are topping 2 billion. What we are witnessing is no less than the complete transformation of social global boundaries at its most fundamental levels. And yet compared to what is still to come from hereon in, it is trifling. In total the world sales estimate for information computer technology tops

3 trillion dollars. The total number of computer companies serving this segment is 800,000 and yet the changes occur so fast that these numbers may be woefully obsolete by the time you read them.

This digital revolution is not only fed by information processing technology but will be significantly spiked by the scientific knowledge base.

In addition to the vast proliferation of information technology tools there is also a vast increase in what is known as "K" tools or knowledge tools to allow us to generate incremental knowledge at a rate never previously experienced. The vast array of Internet and web scientists have access to and share scientific information freely. Virtual walk-around inside a grain of rice is the exciting research that occupies the research labs, for example. Scientists are encouraged, through smart advertisements in scientific magazines to automate their research. Roche Applied Science use this clever caption to sell their knowledge based products: "Process virtually any sample material to isolate DNA, RNA, mRNA and viral nucleic acids in less than two hours using....". Another clever ad from AB Applied Biosystems touts that their DNA analyzer "Will get you there faster".

Not only are we building faster and faster knowledge tools, but we are, at the same time, building faster manufacturing, sophisticated tools to build these knowledge tools. These are two industries growing in tandem and both are multi-billion-dollar industries.

The faster tools, more scientists, instant communication combined with unprecedented knowledge sharing is changing the science landscape itself. Some subjects like time travel, cyborgs, immortality, anti-gravity devices, computer chip-knowledge brain implants, and artificial intelligence were previously taboo subjects for serious scientists but are now freely discussed by these self-same scientists. Not only are these subjects freely talked about, but some of the largest corporations in the world are spending millions of dollars to research them as viable business opportunities.

Imagine, for example, what it means to the knowledge-based economies of the future to be able to help parents that want biologically enhanced smart children. How much are the parents willing to pay for such an advantage? Surely these kids will become the leaders of the new world. On the flipside consider what social and political implications will arise from these treatments? No one can tell for sure where all these earthshaking breakthroughs will lead us, and which ones will be practical and profitable. Doubtless, many will lead to a dead end, but even if only one proves to be a commercial success story it will lead to undreamed wealth and a fundamental reshape of the society in which we live. It would be a mistake to think that all this lofty enlightened view of future technologies as standalone technologies would all be beneficial but certainly the convergence of these will exponentially enhance the value and benefits to the economy.

It's pretty certain from all the signs we've seen that an economic revolution is under way and the new economy arising from the ashes of the collapsed industrial revolution will overshadow the wealth that was generated in the previous industrial revolution. But vast wealth is not the objective in the new economy, for in order for our humanity to move forward from hereon in we will have to do things differently from the past.

We'll have to keep a few things in mind:

1. Unbridled consumerism is no longer the goal
2. We must eliminate the extremes of vast wealth and extreme poverty
3. We must invite the entire world to become equal partners in the unfoldment of the new economy
4. We must eliminate wars except those that are fought to liberate any country or region from aggression by others and provide peace and security everywhere.

5. We must share all that the world produces, equally, with the rest of the world.

It will be a challenge to shed our old ways, for in a past age religiosity as one of its teachings rewarded hard work, thrift and virtue with wealth and prosperity, without giving equal time that this hard work is also service to humanity and a contribution to the public good, which in the end is far more satisfying to the soul.

WEALTH

Wealth is not new. We've been producing wealth in one form or another for millennia. That's good in a way but what has happened over the millennia is that we've also developed a large disparity for the accumulated wealth that is generated by all of humanity and is now being held in fewer and fewer hands. By the way, wealth is not only monetary wealth, but also anything that satisfies your needs or desires. Through the ages we've learned that by accumulating economic surpluses we were enabled to put some of our excesses aside "for a rainy day" as the old saying goes. Wealth has a future but its meaning needs to be redefined to include all of humanity, nobody can be left behind and if some in the society in which we live cannot partake in the generated wealth the rest of us must come to their aid. That will be the meaning of justice in the new economy. Wealth itself has no guilt. What matters is who owns the wealth. Gabriel Zaid, the famous Mexican author, said:" Wealth, above all is an accumulation of possibilities." Aristotle regarded all the pursuit of wealth as unnatural, except for the barest self-sufficiency. Today's new environmental fundamentalist's mantra professes "voluntary simplicity" and views consumerism as a curse and wealth as an abomination. But wealth in its most philosophical sense is good, such as health, love and happiness; you can't have too much of it. Even though that kind of wealth cannot fit in your wallet, few will deny that these are forms of good wealth. Unfortunately, in today's terms we've come to view wealth in its most narrow sense as financial possessions. "Wealth is anything that can satisfy a craving" says Alvin and Heidi Toffler in their book revolutionary wealth (Page 14). It can provide us with some form of satisfaction, and it can be traded for other forms of wealth. Some religions view monetary wealth as an evil impediment, while others preach that hard work and thriftiness will culminate in wealth and God will help in fulfilling your needs and desires. According to Deng Xiaoping in the 1970's, at the start of the Chinese Industrial rebirth was quoted as saying that: "to get rich is glorious". When Deng Xiaoping became the leader of an impoverished China, after Mao Zedong's failed disastrous Cultural Revolution, Deng implemented common sense principles to liberalize the Chinese economy little by little while attempting to maintain a strong centrally controlled Communist state. History can now reflect upon this strategy and call it an unbridled success story, although it has left China with an environmental catastrophe.

Tomorrow's wealth generation will be different from the previous wealth systems. Where the first generation was based on growing things and the second was based on growing things plus making things, now we will experience wealth that is largely based on making knowledge-based things. We will become infinitely smarter because of it and hopefully we will use this panacea of knowledge to live happier and healthier lives. Wealth generation in the new economy demands greater transparency. Nothing will be more important than to know who gets what and this will hopefully lead to the most revolutionary change we will experience.

BUSINESS

B usiness gurus are complaining that business today is moving too fast, so fast in fact that companies are not even bothering with long term strategy. Oddly enough the experts are agreeing that what is needed during these times is not strategy but agility, for if companies are flexible enough, they will survive. Eventually, of course, long-term strategy is vital because in the long run the future will belong to those companies inside and outside of America with a firm company strategy in place; as long as these companies maintain the flexibility required to move with consumer's massive fickleness. Apple Corporation, the world's largest and best-known company, is a prime example of a company that is staying ahead of the business curve. In fact, the reason for their success as a business model is because they have been dictating, for more than a generation now, the business appetite of an eager apple-consumer family. Unfortunately for them they have now reached the middle of their Bell curve and are in danger of ceding their exalted position to other companies that have accepted the Apple model and made it better through imitation, innovation and price performance. Today there is not one business model, which for a certainty can predict the consumer's sustained demand for a particular product or technology. There is far too much choice, and technology evolves too fast and consumer's tastes are too desultory to make long-term predictions about the customer's next choice of favourite computer game or which cell phone, Apple or Samsung, they will buy. There are, of course, ways that consumers are coerced into suddenly liking that new Superman movie that is coming out or playing Pokémon. Some entertainment companies have it down to a fine art.

One of the largest business opportunities is news information. News and information are and will continue to be big business. Many information companies; CNN, Reuters, Bloomberg, CNBC, BBC have made billions spewing out news of every kind. From earthquakes and tsunamis to the latest interest hike by the Feds it is all eagerly anticipated and in some cases millions of dollars are made or lost based on the latest stock market report. No one can really understand how these media companies are able to exert such influence, but the fact is that they do. It seems that it is not only the news but also the way the news is presented. When the Apple chairman is quoted that their company is doing fine due to its adherence to "sound business fundamentals" and even though the Apple stock price dropped by 30.00 dollars that day, stockholders tended to believe him. But when a report comes out that a hurricane in Chile has devastated the countries' fruit crop, the New York stock exchange, reacts negatively and all the stock prices tumble for that day. It's all in the language and phrases like "sound business fundamentals" tend to calm the market and words like hurricanes ruining the fruit crop or a rate increase in the interest rate will spook the markets around the world. Words are used not only to report but also to confound an unsuspecting audience. "Economics has its own inerrantists" says Alvin Toffler: *Revolutionary Wealth pge. 25*. The economists claim its business as usual and nothing could be better, all in the face of confusing and contradictory evidence. They state, further, that the economy has only been minimally affected by the new knowledge-based economy and "fundamentals are sound".

The codification of the language of business took more than a generation to evolve to its incomprehensible end to most of us. It has as its aim to puzzle and confound the great unwashed and the key to DE- codification is firmly locked away. Terms like "Credit Default Swaps, Credit Derivatives and Tranche" are terms only the insiders understand. The best that we can do is to use reliable trustworthy professionals for our financial wealth generation and stick to the fundamentals. The rest is just noise.

Of course, during the Industrial Age, Central banks and the Federal Reserve played key roles in the creation of wealth and we witnessed the devastating effects at the height of the credit crisis in 2008 when credit was withheld by the central banks and the entire world economy came crashing down. The new economy may no longer be so dependent on central bank financing and many of the banking functions will be carried out automatically through the electronic infrastructure now being set in place.

And then there is Bitcoin the promise of the future economy: the promise of a world without banks. It's basic in its concept but not easy to understand because the language sounds foreign with ideas that are not easily understood: Bitcoin is digital currency, created and held electronically and not in a bank or locker or safe. No one is in control of Bitcoin. It is not printed currency, like dollars or euros. It is money that is known as crypto currency produced by individual people, and hopefully businesses, and generated on computers worldwide, using software that solves mathematical problems. You can download a myriad of math solvers for free which will give you the necessary tools to verify that your bitcoin is real and not fake. Bitcoin is used to buy things on your computer electronically. In essence, it is no different from buying your things using dollars, yen, or euros; those currencies are also traded digitally. The big difference in the use of bitcoin versus regular currency is that it is not traded in a central location, i.e. a bank. Thus, no single institution can control the bitcoin network and it, at the same time, bypasses the scrutiny of governments and other organizations that like to know and control what you're doing.

It is rumored that the inventor of the bitcoin protocol is someone by the name of Satoshi Nakamoto. He published a paper in 2008 outlining the protocol and in 2009 released the first version of the software. He participated with others on the fine-tuning of the software and then faded from the project in 2010. The software although brilliant as it is, remains open source and Nakamoto never revealed anything personal about himself so we're not even sure if he (she) is a real person. The algorithm that makes the bitcoin software work so brilliantly cannot really be attributed to Nakamoto since it seems that it was merely a clever pseudonym.

Since bitcoin is electronic currency it need not be printed and held in a central location. It is created digitally by a group of people, anyone can join, and used by the participants over and over. Bitcoin is supposedly simple in that it is, easy to set up and its anonymous it is also completely transparent since every transaction that has ever used that bitcoin is attached in a version of a general ledger called the blockchain which tells all except the name and addresses of the participants who have ever used the bitcoin. Anther important feature that makes it so attractive is its speed, you can send money anywhere in the world and it is there minutes later. The only drawback there is no return of the funds even if you change your mind.

SPEED OF THE NEW BUSINESS

I n the new information age, the speed at which business is conducted and undergoes rapid change will be a fundamental business tool. It is evident, based on the rhetoric in the American worker
community, that the average American worker has not come to
terms with the reality that "Business as usual" is now a thing of the
past. We cannot go back to the way business was conducted in the
past. The very first thing we need to do is gain an informed understanding of the way business must go forward. The reality is that
business cannot move at one speed and the understanding of the
consequences of a business decision that is vital and must be made
in a timely fashion, operates at a slower speed. Alvin Toffler refers
to this phenomenon as the "de-synchronization effect" and it refers
to one of the most fundamental tools in business: Time itself. Many
business CEO's in America understood the need for speed and
business school guru Milton Friedman, professor emeritus at the
famed Chicago school of economics urged as an instant response,
"Be first! Be agile! Shoot now, aim later!" *Alvin Toffler, Revolutionary
Wealth p 46.* It turned out that this simplistic advice could be no

further from the truth as it led to shoddy, low quality products and unhappy angry customers. It is a prime example that shows that business and the changing economies of the world were clearly out of sync and at the same time produced a period of agonizing adjustment and great bewilderment. Fortunately, now America, Canada, Europe and China all boast advanced economies where every institution operating within these economies is supposed to operate at the same speed. It seems apparent that some of these institutions are not online yet and if perchance they are, they have not been able to synchronize their schedules. It is for that reason that the old industrial based infrastructures around the world are slowing their own progress towards a knowledge-based economy. The North American workers working in the few remaining North American assembly-line factories are perhaps the last participants in the new economy who have not been able to come to terms with the way commerce is evolving, not of their own volition since they are still awaiting a "new deal' to be brokered through their unions; a deal that will never come to fruition. The unions still have a role to play to provide protection for its membership, to ensure that the workers and the company get a fair deal while at the same time the need to ensure, for their own survival, that they remain current viable and on the cutting edge of the new economy.

The jury is still out to determine which institution in the North American economy will be fully prepared to engage the new economy. Will it be government or business? There is much at stake here, for not only are we attempting to adapt and accommodate, and we still have a 'winner take all and take no prisoners" attitude with the emerging nations, China and India who also have a "take no prisoners mentality". We've come to terms, I think, that we are no longer hewers of water and we realize that no matter how cheaply our factories can turn out widgets, the factories in China can turn them out cheaper. We also have come to realize that punitive tariffs that we can impose on our competitors from

China, Korea, and Japan... in this new global economy will just further complicate doing reciprocative commerce with our trading partners. Some North American, not all, get it: Fedex, in the early eighties, ran a brilliant campaign which underscored the new way of doing business with a slogan; "When it absolutely, positively has to be there overnight." and Oracle "moving data at the speed of business" are two effective examples of the urgency needed to be competitive in the new economy.

It seems clear that amongst all the participants of the new economy, government seems to be the slowest to change; for example: It typically take years for governments to enlarge airports and build that extra runway even though it was needed yesterday, or for the food and drug administration to test and approve a new life saving drug even as people are dying of the disease. Our infra structure, particularly the roadways and bridges badly need repairs and upgrades, but the government decision making is so slow that these repairs are not done citing lack of money. It is imperative, in order to be competitive and successful in the new economy, to "operate at the speed of business". It is something so basic that it is taught in all the business schools in the very first term of the first year.

EDUCATION

Especially in the new knowledge base economy a disciplined well-educated workforce is vitally important to sustaining growth and to remain competitive in the world. Education is the key to success. Some countries are better than others. In North America we've always thought that our educational system is one of the best in the world. Periodically these assumptions are put to the test.

When the OECD's (Organization for Economic Cooperation and Development) comprehensive world education ranking report came out the United States did not do so well. It ranked 14th in the world, a long way below many of the European countries.

The results are interesting, and it is based on a standard rigorous and comprehensive way of measuring a countries' access to basic knowledge which includes adult literacy levels, enrolment in primary and secondary school levels including women's access to education. These criteria determine which countries provide better educational opportunities for their citizens.

Top 20 countries 2015/2016 (Source OECD)

- South Korea
  Japan and South Korea compete fiercely for 1st rank. Koreans defeated Japan on 3 levels. Despite heavily investing in childhood education Japan is no#2 in some levels. Children in South Korea attend school seven-day a week. The national education budget estimated last year was $11,300,000,000. The literacy rate is total 97.9% out of which males are sharing 99.2% and 96.6% of females.
  The GDP (PPP) per capita estimated in 2014 is $34,795.
- Japan
  The technology-based educational structure has provided the nation with some great figures in the knowledge and insight.
  The GDP nearly 5.96 trillion USD is well evident to prove the claim.
- Singapore
  The strong and highly ranked primary education system is none less than 3rd rank in the competition.
  The GDP (PPP) per capita is U$D 64,584 is also number 3rd in the world.
- Hong Kong
  The school education management is pretty much in the way as UK model of education. The educational budget for the last year was $39, 420 per capita. The primary, secondary and higher education levels are exemplary in their approach and work. English and Cantonese Chinese are the mainstream languages for educational texts. The literacy rate is 94.6%.
  The GDP (PPP) per capita accumulated in 2014 is $404.892 billion.
- Finland
  The old champion is loosing ground to it´s Asian rivals. A number of folks still consider Finland as no#1as the best

educational system which exactly isn't the fact anymore. The premature child admission is a big drawback in the system. The no tuition fees system has an annual educational budget of €11.1 billion.

The country's Gross domestic product was $36,395 per capita (2014).

- UK

With the devolution of the Education system in the UK, the individual governments are administrating matters relating to education on their own. The Scottish, Welsh, Northern Irish and English governments are minding and administering their educational systems on an individual basis instead of a collective under the kingdom's unified standards. The Pearson has ranked UK second in the European ranks and #6 in the worldwide rankings in their 2014 publication. Oddly enough the Scottish system has a slight edge over England's when it comes to comparative competitiveness.

The GDP per capita is 21st highest in the world at $38,711.

- Canada

English and French are the official languages. The literacy rate is 99% for both male and female. College graduation is the highest in the world percentage wise. Education is compulsory up to the age of 16.

GDP per Capita: $44,656 and Canada invests 5.4% of its Gross Domestic Product in the education sector.

- Netherlands

The low investments, weak planning and management of the education system in the high school sector, have put Netherland 8th in the world ranking.

GDP per Capita: $42,586

- Ireland

The literacy rate is 99% for male and female alike. Education is free from primary to university level.

Ireland spends 8.759 billion euro annually education.

- Poland
  The Polish ministry of education is in charge of the countries' education system at all levels. Poland is ranked #10 in the world
  GDP per Capita: $21,118
- Denmark
  Denmark's educational system consists of Pre-school, primary, secondary, higher and adult education. The secondary education system is further divided into gymnasium, higher preparatory, higher commercial, and higher technical and vocational education programmes. Education is compulsory up to the age of 16. The post-secondary education isn't mandatory, however an impressive 82% of the students are enrolled in post-secondary education. Denmark's world ranking is #11
  GDP per Capita: $57,998
- Germany
  Germany is dedicated to developing one of the best educational systems in the world. Education is fully State funded. Primary and secondary education is compulsory. German universities, although free to everyone, are among the world's best institutions of learning and among the best in Europe.
  GDP per Capita: $41,248
  World ranking is #12
- Russia
  Much can be done to improve the primary education system. Russia spends about 20 billion USD annually on education.
  World ranking is #13
  GDP per Capita: $14,645
- United States
  The US, as the strongest economy in the world lags behind in their educational system. Their world ranking is a

disappointing #14. The $1.3 trillion national educational budget is among one of the highest in the world. The literacy rate is 99% for both male & female. 85% of the students have attained a secondary school diploma, while only 30% of those go on to a post secondary education, which is not free.

GDP per Capita: $54,980

KNOWLEDGE

How important is knowledge in the evolving information economy? If we say that it is the most important thing then we need to classify the level of knowledge. Is knowledge smartness? Is more knowledge better than less? What type of knowledge is better, theoretical or applied? Human knowledge sets us apart from the rest of the animal kingdom and puts us at the top of the heap because of it. Not only do we have more knowledge, but we are able to apply that knowledge much better than the rest of the animal kingdom. Because of our exalted position as masters of our own domain, on earth anyways, does it give us special privileges? What is our responsibility towards the other animals? Are we their caretakers? In our short history as Homo Sapiens what have we accomplished? As powerful as we are and accountable to no one all we've done thus far is to wreak havoc on our environment and as caretakers of the earth we've killed off more species of animals, created a natural catastrophe.

In a knowledge-based society there will always be more questions than answers. "Why", is a legitimate question. The amount of knowledge a human being possesses is not the only measure of a man. If you know more than all the other people in the room does not elevate you to smartest person if the knowledge you have does not come with a plan to put that knowledge to work in the service of humanity, for without purpose knowledge is meaningless. The question that most people have, now and in the future, is whether the entities with Artificial Knowledge (AI) that are coming online will render Homo Sapiens subservient and obsolete? If the answer to that question is yes, then we need to make plans for this not to happen. The reason why is that humans have been put on this earth with a mission, one that to some has been clearly spelled out and to others is merely fantasy. I think we can all agree that we have been put here for no purposeful function and it is up to us to find out what our mission and purpose are. It is self evident that AI entities of the future will know much more that our best scientists but does that render our scientists inferior to the machines they helped design and develop. When is a machine smarter than its developer? We possess an ingredient that machines will never possess and that is heart, the mitigating, altruistic self-regulating instrument that renders knowledge purposeful in a human way. Can we build the humanity into that AI entity and make it superior to who we are? Can the created become smarter than the creator? That special characteristic which defines who we are. The thing that makes us cry at the birth of a child, appreciate the beauty of a sunset, an area of a Puccini opera, laugh at a joke, skinny dip in the neighbour's pool, love your children and hate your job. Everything that makes us human and that really make no sense, except to us gives us hope and joy for the future. We hope that better things will come and the belief that a greater entity we call God is guiding our steps. And yet, with all that, we still have the option to say no to it all, if we so wish. That is the knowledge that cannot be replaced by the smartest AI entity which will ever be built and that is a million times smarter than we will ever be. After all it will simply be a tool to us to use as we wish. To build such an entity will require a lot of though and consultation with precise guidelines of what we want these entities to do for us. One thing is clear; we must build them so that they will always stay subservient to us. To make sense we must be able to find purpose for all knowledge, use it in a sentence, apply it in a practical way for the betterment of our daily existence.

The essence of the knowledge source remains a mystery to us and all we have to go on are the inherent qualities of the knowledge we gather to apply it in some constructive way for the public good. This gives the knowledge some reason for its discovery. We're all intricate parts of the bigger entity, yet to be defined, in some generic way. All that we know is that we're all related in some way and I firmly believe that being an integral part of the family of man matters and is what sets us apart from AI entities no matter how smart these entities will become.

I believe that it is unlikely that we, Homo Sapiens, will become subordinate to the AI entities we will have created even if they are a million times smarter, for they will always lack the sentient sensibilities that helps define our humanity.

Changes sweeping across the world and affecting every aspect of our daily lives are now creating the most fundamental shifts in wealth generation and establishing simultaneously a new timetable for the evolvement of the new information age. Let's hope that this new era will bring with it a more just society, one in which we can all live in peace and prosperity.

LOW INTEREST RATES

The fundamentals of the new economy include low interest rates in order to drive the economies of the world forward. This is the opinion of all the players; corporations, central banks and investors all around the world. Even though all are on the same page, cracks are starting to develop. China watchers are warning that China could suffer a financial meltdown similar to the one that hit Japan in 1997 and worse, that an environmental crisis will have worldwide consequences, destabilizing the global economy for years to come. The convergence of these problems plus an energy crisis and another outbreak of disease like SARS could throw the entire world economy into a recession. The system is fragile and on life support. Nothing is allowed to go wrong. China's struggles affect us all and are happening against a backdrop of Chinese discontented factory workers and peasants alike. This is all happening at a time when the burgeoning Chinese middle class is flexing its muscle. They are increasingly nationalistic and confident that they, not their parents or the factory workers, or the peasants are the way of the future for China. According to historical events the central government in China has been successful in blocking large-scale political uprising by any group, whether they be workers, peasants, students or quasi-political groups like Falun Gong, but its ability is quickly dissipating. What follows could be a change of the old guard.

The ultimate loser in the worldwide financial game of "chicken" is predicated on the idea that the one who blinks first loses. This means that nobody is interested to move the interest rate up. Except that there will be no winners this time. Because it is a global game and we're all inextricably connected to one another. We can trip each other up, sorry everyone else can trip up the United States, particularly China and Russia, since they hold the majority of America's debt and by calling the loans or selling American dollars because they have lost faith in the American greenback would also cost China the most important trading partner they have. It's a stalemate for now and that's probably a good thing until we can figure out a better scenario.

At the crossroad of change China finds itself in the improbable situation where given the right circumstances could sweep aside the current leadership and give rise to a more benevolent charismatic leadership. No longer a Communist leadership or a capitalist leadership, but in a country that hungers to replace Mao's near religion of Marxism with a system of government that gathers together the needs of all its people, peasants, factory workers and young new wave element people under a "religious" emblem. In a country not tolerant of religion, many religions and quasi religions abound, particularly in the countryside. The New York Times estimates that nearly 200 million Chinese are regular or casual followers of a variety of faiths from Christianity to obscure sects...they are the Roman Catholics, Baptist, Lutheran and a myriad other Christian denominations and the Crying faction and the Spirit Church, the Holistic church and the Shouters, the Disciple Association and White Sun. Some are apocalyptic and strongly anti-communist.

Two obscure sects are The Eastern Lightning and Three Grades of Servants who claim millions of members. Imagine these fanatical groups in charge, with their finger poised on the nuclear button. This nightmare scenario might seem farfetched but remember this is China with a long history of different masters in charge. China is resilient and it has developed into a contemporary affluent world power. It has an opportunity to demonstrate to the rest of the world that it has the capacity and the willingness to develop into a modern world power that considers the betterment of all its people, something that other world powers have been unable to do in their own economies because the deeply entrenched vested interest of the one percenters; those that are in charge and are not willing to give up their billions or the reigns of power.

HOPE FOR THE FUTURE?

As we move forward into the new age, we find that there is plenty to be worried about. The list is horrible and endless: The possibility of war between The United States and practically "everybody else"; the possibility of war between Israel and practically "everybody else" in the Middle East; the possibility of war between Iran and practically "everybody else"; the possibility of war between North Korea and South Korea; the possibility of war between Mainland China and Taiwan; Terrorist attacks around the globe; Pandemics; Earthquakes; Hurricanes and of course global warming. All of these are worry-some but we must realize that many of these fears are in themselves "fashionable" and it makes them no less dangerous but we've always lived under some kind of doomsday scenario; remember the cold war and the Cuban missile crisis and we were sure worried about them. It caused a paralyzing fear. Far from stopping us from moving forward into the new age we should, instead, look at the future with anticipation, for the future is bright with the promise of new and smart devices that will think for themselves and with a minimum of input will make life more pleasant. We are waxing nostalgic for the good old days where a job meant security in the knowledge that you would have the same job from the beginning of our working career until retirement with a good pension. Yet we are being pushed forward into the new age without knowing what we'll be doing and where we'll be working at jobs not yet invented, probably changing careers multiple times in our working life. No doubt the upcoming changes will profoundly affect the way we used to do things and cause major shifts in earning capacity and wealth creation, but it is something we will all have to live through. These challenges will require problem- solving techniques beyond what we know today even the experts don't seem to agree on what the next step is. It all depends on how we chose to view the pending changes and how confident we are that the new tomorrow will not be that much different from the old yesterday. What seems to exacerbate the problem is the phenomenal economic rise of China and India and their unceasing demands for more energy to drive their economies particularly at a time when the cost keeps going up.

THE INFORMATION AGE EXPLAINED

I n order to successfully enter the new information age, the greatest challenge will be to integrate the old world with the new world while at the same time synchronize our thinking from the very large "Einstein universe" called classical existence with the infinitesimally small quantum universe called quantum existence. We've learned that the theory and the problem solving in classical existence, where the theories of Einstein neatly apply to all that we've come to know $(E=Mc2)$ are not compatible with quantum existence and yet we will have to solve the problem and make them compatible one to the other. In other words; what is true in the world of the very large must also be true in the quantum universe, there can be no contradictions. We exist in the universe of the very, very large and so we've come to know it quite well. We've designed methods of communications that lets us know one another better, our desires, passion, love and sadness and free will; all these are familiar to us. Are these same qualities true in quantum existence or are they like all other things in the quantum reality, deconstructed so that we do not yet know how to apply these characteristics there. We now have to find a mathematical formula that will solve the mysteries in quantum existence as well as classical existence without the two conflicting with one another. It will be an algorithm that suffices all conditions, such as "the Schrödinger cat in the box is both alive and dead in the box, at the same time". Traveling faster than the speed of light and go beyond time and space while remaining an "entity intact" and separating body and soul and reconstituting it simultaneously. It is clear that some of these cannot be attained in only one reality since we are, in order to accomplish this, operating in at least two different realities, and maybe more than two. The biggest question of all will need to be answered:" If we do all this and can create sentient life that replicates our own existence in the minutest detail, are we then God?" The answer; not really since we are only replicating what God has done before us and the created cannot become the Creator. The most we can say is that we are perfect "creator imitators".

We need to do all this if we want to reach the ultimate goal and create "Sentient Artificial Intelligence" (SAI), entities who are like us in every aspect; that will be the crowning achievement of the information age. The first generation of AI entities will be quite rudimentary in that they will not look like us, nor will they have any ability to think and act for themselves, except in a very mechanical way. These SAI's are entities that have feelings and opinions and free will so that they can perfect themselves if they so desire, just like us. To most of us the quantum world does not relate to this existence in any discernible way and yet they co-exist. When we talk about an algorithm that will do all this, it is clear that we will have to do the Creating Algorithm (CA) in multiple stages, introducing them as we resolve one issue at a time. The other big challenge the algorithm will have to accomplish is to solve the problem of finding a way back to this reality if any separation of body and soul takes place. The bigger challenge, after we have accomplished all this, is to yield to the sentient AI entities for their much greater knowledge while at the same time face the risk that these entities may very well take over the role of "masters of the universe" from us while relegating us to the role of servants to them. That would be the ultimate irony, so how do we stop that from happening? How far do we allow AI existence to develop in a supporting role and still remain the undisputed masters over them and at the same time let them become much smarter than we are? The idea of being servants to our own creation is not a particularly appealing one, so we'll have to design the AI entities with certain missing characteristics that we possess. One of these and perhaps the most important one is free will. If we design free will into their architecture it will, out of necessity and based on the exigencies outlined have to be subordinated to our free will. Subservience to us will need to be built in to their "character". If we do not do this then we run the risk that the AI entities will assume a role which will enable them to figure out that in order for them to progress to achieve their greatest potential they will have to remove us from the role as masters over them, for they will be infinitely smarter than we are.

THE EMPATHIC CIVILIZATION

How do we know that the new Information Age will take hold? It is inevitable that we are moving towards this new era, but it would be quite impossible if humankind had not been made ready for this radical transformation. It requires a new universal vision for it to take hold. It requires empathy. Empathy is the ability to feel with others. Commerce up until now has always been done with the competitive "Take no prisoners" attitude, a "winner take all" view; one that espouses the view that competition is good as long as there is a winner and that winner better be me. As the world has shrunk, not in size but in its ability for instant communication transfer through the worldwide web, it becomes virtually impossible to take advantage of the element of surprise or one upmanship in the way we conduct commerce. There are no surprises and the only thing that seems to matter most is to bring goods to market cheaply and efficiently and goods come from everywhere in the world now. Therefore, it is important that we learn a new language, a language of understanding, cooperation, courtesy and honesty. Where to learn this new language is now being offered through the educational systems in the classroom, but it is through the willingness to accept multicultural and sometimes contradictory realities that will empower us to incorporate empathy into our everyday interactions with others. The new classroom is the world in which we live. We learn that the world is stressed and that we need to conserve energy and that the family automobile is wasteful in its energy consumption and its emissions the prime cause of carbon dioxide into the atmosphere. We also learned that fossil fuel use is heating up the earth's temperature which causes less rainfall, more draughts, which adversely affects food production all in one lesson. Of course, I exaggerate because this knowledge is coming to us as we become increasingly aware that business as usual is no longer business as usual and that drastic changes need to occur to save the world and all that is therein. Ever greater consumption of the earth's resources culminates into a dramatic deterioration of our planet's health and it is for that reason that we need to cultivate a global empathy in this now highly interconnected world as we are battling for the earth's very existence.

It is ironic that the chroniclers of human history seem to have no feelings of empathy when they write about social conflict and wars and as they describe the misdeeds of evildoers and the heroic acts of our great men. They write, dispassionately, about economic injustice and the redress of social grievances. Nor do they seem to have any thoughts about the evolution of human affection and the resultant impact on society or culture. I guess it is because they only report history and are careful not to draw any conclusions, for they do not wish to skew social trends through biased observations.

Georg Wilhelm Fredrich Hegel the German philosopher remarked that happiness is "the blank pages of history" because they are "periods of harmony" and happy people live out their lives in a make-believe world of familial relations and happy social affiliations. The discontented and disgruntled are not of those; they are often more interested in exercising control and restoring justice. Much of history is about the abnormal condition and exercise of power.

Even though much of our daily interaction is empathic, simply because we are so inclined, we have been trained from birth to be competitive and that means that we suppress our empathic feelings most of the time. Particularly in sports, empathy is a characteristic that gets in the way of winning. It does create social life and is an emissary of an ever-advancing civilization, even though it has not been given the attention it needs as the cause for a kinder gentler world. Empathy is derived from sympathy, but empathy conjures up the image of active involvement in the condition of others. The popularization of empathy has been coined in phrases such as "I feel your pain" used by former president Bill Clinton and others such "I feel with you" "Someone knows what it's like to be me" …

Researchers have determined that it is not only human beings who possess the capacity for empathy and that all animals possess this capacity. This critical assessment is borne from extensive observation of all animal behaviour.

It may well be the characteristic that will enable us, in the new information age, to discern the difference between us human beings and the coming of sentient artificial intelligent entities.

Formal education in schools' systems in the United States and elsewhere have now incorporated empathic attunement in the nascent field of teaching emotional intelligence, suggesting that it is an important emotional marker in the child's mental development. These educational advances are helping to nurture a much-needed social sensibility for the coming information age.

Adam Smith, the Scottish political economist and philosopher, achieved fame through his highly influential book "Inquiry into the nature and Causes of the wealth of nations (1776)". Smith was the son of the comptroller of the customs at Kirkcaldy, Fife, Scotland. He wrote: *"every individual is continually exerting himself to find out the most advantageous employment for whatever capital he can command. It is his own advantage, indeed, and not that of society, which he has in view. But the study of his own advantage naturally, or rather necessarily, leads him to prefer that employment which is most advantageous to the society...*" In this day and age this view is no longer as relevant as it was in 1776 or 1976. The Information Age has changed all that. The notion that all transactions should be transparent has replaced the assumption that business transactions must be purely made because of self-interest.

We human beings are, firstly, social animals who seek others' companionship and use empathetic emotions to transcend themselves and find meaning and purpose in the relationship with others. How do we then account for the indescribable violence we heap onto one another? How do we explain the rape we inflict on the earth we inhabit? We are the only creatures who have left such a destructive footprint. It is unexplainable and yet there may be an explanation: at the core of our existence there is a duality, a paradox that demonstrates our need to be destroyers of our own environment but, historically, also be the builders of great societies. As we progressed from a forager/hunter tribal existence to an agricultural/hunter existence we carved out territorial/migratory space for ourselves and as our tribal way of life was supplanted by communal/village/city societies we pushed back the jungle that surrounded us; often in detrimental excessive ways and destroying everything in its path. In our efforts for "civilizing" our surroundings we've clearly gone too far and it is now time to repair and rebuild what we have wrought, hence the need for an enlightened, empathetic life from hereon in. In this effort no one can be left behind for it is that, for example, the paucity of Africa reflects poorly on the rest of the world. Our new empathic civilization must share, equally, what the biosphere produces, without exception. Nothing else will do. It is for that very reason that we must construct an all-inclusive world, a commonwealth of independent, autonomous nations bound together by a common cause and one world governing body.

The turnabout to morph from a strictly ego driven world to the empathic civilization we envision comes at the very moment when the emerging nations of India, China, Brazil, Bangladesh, Vietnam and the Philippines are sucking up the last remaining resources and unbalancing our own complex and interdependent North American and the E.U economies and stressing the biosphere to its maximum at the same time. We are starting to ask the right questions in the face of this new reality: Can we continue to sustain ourselves? It is because of that question and others that we are starting the frightening thought that we might not make it and that we will become extinct as a species. The voracious global economy is threatening to overwhelm nature and its ability to cope with the rapid human induced climate change. The general understanding of the end game is a six-degree rise in the earth's temperature resulting in the demise of our world as we know it.

The contradiction at the heart of the human destiny is to understand the relationship we have with the planet. We must step back from the abyss and contemplate a plan of action, which is both sustainable, while it does, at the same time serve the needs of all the people on earth in a fair and equitable manner. It will mean that inevitably, we will have to do with much less. Yet the change will occur with the realization that empathic consciousness must trump the egocentric sense of selfhood.

Jeremy Rifkin in his book "The Empathic Civilization says:" Empathy *becomes the thread that weaves an increasingly differentiated and individualized population into an integral social tapestry, allowing the social organism to function as a whole.*" It sounds to me like the inevitability of life's natural progression on this earth, that, whether we choose to or not, we are on the path of a united humanity; one in our fight for personal survival and one in our wish to live a rich social life where no one is left behind. In other words, we take care of each other with the knowledge that we all matter.

In the past industrial age, the brilliant success of it was based on someone figuring out that the *"consumer capitalism is due in large part to the eroticization of desires and sexualisation of consumption."* Jeremy Rifkin, *The Empathic civilization p.48*

Madison Avenue Advertising used the same tactic of erotic appeal to advertise cars, kitchen-wares, and all different goods some not so sexy and it worked wonderfully well.

At the other end of the spectrum we must consider the pronouncements of Sigmund Freund, the great Psychologist of the 19th and 20th century who is often referred to as the one who defined human nature. He subscribed to the notion of man's fallen, depraved and materialistic nature, framing it with the idea *"that all that drives man is his insatiable libido and that sexual relations is the focal point of his life and all external reality becomes merely instrumental to achieving sexual release"*. His thoughts, so evocative and powerful, reverberated so well with the public that it has continued, to this day, to define the human story. It has had dire consequences in the way we parent our children, the way we conduct ourselves in business and the way we enact the body politic. Man is often depicted *"as a savage beast to whom consideration towards his own kind is something alien"* Sigmund Freud, *Civilization and it Discontent, (New York: Norton, 1961) pp.58-9*

Sadly, it is true that more than 60% of all Internet content is made up of sexual content and gambling and this does not bode well for a more enlightened humanity. Freud is dismissive about the Golden Rule that says: "love one's neighbour as oneself."" *...nothing else runs so strongly counter to the original nature of man."* Sigmund Freud, *Civilization and Its Discontent, (New York: Norton, 1961) pp. 58-9*

Freud maintains that society is an expedient compromise in which man has: *"exchanged a portion of his possibilities of happiness for a portion of security." Sigmund Freud, Civilization and Its Discontent, (New York: Norton, 1961) pp. 61-9*

It is paradoxical to think that if it is in man's nature to destroy and kill one another, as Freud posits, how can we account for the fact that life itself seeks more order, integration and togetherness? It was a fact he could not reconcile; the fact that biological organisms and communities seek to want to live in order and security and protect themselves against lawlessness and chaos. If death and destruction are at man's core then it would be at the expense of Darwin's theory of biological evolution which states that all species of organisms arise and develop through the natural selection of small, inherited variations that increase the individual's ability to compete, survive, and reproduce.

It is enigmatic that in Freud's strange analysis of human nature he does not consider the love of a mother for her children as a powerful inducement for empathy. Perhaps, as he explains, in a revealing admission about himself, *"I cannot discover this oceanic feeling in myself" Sigmund Freud, Civilization and Its Discontent, (New York: Norton, 1961) pp. 2-3*

As a further explanation Freud regards the infant as libido driven from the outset and regards the mother as a utility to itself. He poses the interesting question whether the feeling of oneness in infancy might express itself later in life as the need for a religious Godhead but then, in the same breath, dismisses it as most unlikely for the source of a child's feeling of helplessness is present in the longing it evokes for his father. This likely demonstrates Freud's own emotional weak spot; that is the need for religiosity as strictly utilitarian.

Viewed through the lens of history, Freud has failed in his argument for a continuous dominant patriarchal society as we are viewing the end of life of the industrial age and the beginning of the information age. Even though male dominance has, for thousands of years, been at the heart of an ever-evolving society, we now witness the women taking their rightful place alongside men in the industrialized world and there are strong signs of emergence in the developing nations. Employers are pragmatic and do no longer care what sex people are, as it is their goal to hire the brightest, most innovative, energetic people regardless of what sex they are. This paves the way for women to escape centuries of serfdom, slavery and servitude.

A younger generation of psychologists, after Freud, started to pick apart the central tenets of Freud's vision of the human condition. Fittingly the male/female roles have been redefined to be more empathic in the new social order and the emerging information age. The timing of this change may be coincidental to the start of the new age, but it must be kept in mind that the change was inevitable as we are all engaged in carrying forward an ever-advancing civilization. A civilization that is more sympathetic and loving. Since we have now transcended borders through instant communications from anywhere on the planet, we can't help but feel a kinship with all that inhabit this planet. It is now generally accepted by most psychologists that the biological need for nurture in an infant is not a libido driven impulse as maintained by Freud but merely a need for love, companionship and an innate sense of wanting to belong in a progressively more empathic society. In an infant, these feelings start out with play as a most important social activity since it is where we generate companionship, trust, imagination and creativity. Reciprocity in social action is at the heart of any relationship. If reciprocity is withheld the sense of selfhood and sociability is seriously compromised, thus possibly generating a variety of psychopathological conditions. While social theorists are making the argument that babies are pre-wired for sociability and companionship rather than their sexual libido being the driving force in life. It now appears abundantly evident that, after a generation of Freudian thinking has misguided us, the sociability theory wins out.

A mother's traditional role as the main caregiver of her children, might claim her to an existence she wishes to shed. In the new economy that role will be shared, more and more, with others in her family and her community as well as with her husband thus freeing her to become equal partners, unencumbered by any kind of male dominance.

The new awareness about human nature is that it shows human beings in a much more social environment. We don't like loneliness, but love companionship and we are predisposed to show kindness and empathy to others.

It is important to note that we are not the only animals exhibiting sociability traits and empathy. Charles Darwin in his *Origin of the Species* made significant observations in the area of cognitive science as it relates to sociability in evolution. In a later work *The Descent of Man* and in *Expression of the Emotions in Man and Animals* he wrote the following about social nature: "*Every one must have noticed how miserable horses, dogs and sheep are when separated from their companions and what strong mutual affection horses and dogs, at least, show on their reunion.*" *Charles Darwin, The Descent of Man, p. 104.* Darwin also commented on the grooming behaviour of animals. He was intrigued with how "*...social animals perform many services for one another; horses nibble, cows lick each other on any spot that itches. Monkeys search each other for external parasites.*" *Charles Darwin, The Descent of Man, p. 105.*

He was fascinated by the animals' sense of humour" *[d]ogs show what may be fairly called a sense of humour as distinct from mere play. If a bit of a stick or other such object is thrown to one, he will often carry it away for a short distance and then squatting down with it on the ground close before him, will wait until his master comes quite close to take it away. The dog will then seize it and rush away in triumph, repeating the same maneuver and evidently enjoying the practical joke.*" *Charles Darwin, The Descent of Man, p. 71.* Social beings were how Darwin viewed these higher animals, full of emotions and endowed with a capacity to empathize on the plight of others, not only his own kind, but also other animals and human beings. Darwin espoused the view, during the early part of his career, that survival of the fittest was at the root of human survival, but later on, towards the end of his life he came to view human life as "impulses do not always arise from anticipated pleasure." more deeply ingrained than pleasure, he maintains, is a strong social instinct which drives man to commit virtuous and noble acts. In a gripping passage he writes about our sympathetic impulses (the word empathy had not yet been invented) and an age when humanity will stretch its social instincts *"becoming more tender and more widely diffused until they are extended to all sentient beings. As soon as this virtue is honoured and practiced by some few of us it spreads through instruction and example to the young and eventually becomes incorporated in public opinion." Charles Darwin, The Descent of Man, p. 83.*

Many behavioural scientists now believe that play, as an activity, performs the most powerful role in developing empathy as it, at the same time, establishes the capacity for social interaction. Play creates attachment, mindfulness, trust, affection and social bonds that will last a lifetime. When kids are denied play, they will often not develop the social skills for interaction and be distrustful of others. They'll learn to survive but it will often be stressful and confusing for them. Play develops social capacity and allows our imagination to soar. Play connects us by creating real and imagined settings from which we make up life's experiences that will inextricably binds us to others for a lifetime. Friedrich Schiller, the famous German philosopher, wrote in his *On the Aesthetic Education of Man,* in 1795 *"man plays only when he is in the fullest sense of the word a human being, and he is fully a human being when he plays." Friedrich Schiller, On the Aesthetic Education of Man, pp. 27-68*

One of the most important aspects of the nature/nurture debate is that it is still going on with neither side a definite winner over the other. The challenge is that we're not sure yet whether a child is predisposed in his DNA to certain traits it has inherited from his parents or whether he or she is influenced by life's experiences and the environment in which the child is raised. All we can say is that the child is becoming self-conscious with its own unique personality and the ability to discern the difference between fantasy and reality and certainly both nature and nurturing play important roles in human development but we can't say with a certainty that one is of greater importance than the other. It is quite evident that the empathy the child cultivates early on is dependent on the relationship it observes between his parents. The empathy thusly cultivated is of great importance. It opens the child's mind to the social and emotional world that surrounds him and is the impetus for the warmth and affection the child will show forth in the future. The answer to which of the two is more important, nature or nurture, can only be answered through close observation since it is the intimate bond and emotional relationships the child forges with its parents or caregivers that will encode patterns of behaviour that will stay with it throughout the child's life. Stanley Greenspan, a clinical professor of psychiatry at George Washington University Medical School answers the dichotomy in an elegant way *"[c]onsciousness develops from this continuous interaction in which biology organizes experience and experience organizes biology.[W]hat we mean is the ability to experience the most basic emotions in ourselves and others and to reflect on these in the context of our families, society, culture and environment." Dr. Stanley Greenspan, The Origins of Consciousness, Morality and Intelligence, p.113-4*

FURTHER READING

Martin Gilens and Benjamin I. Page; *Testing Theories of American Politics: Elites, Interest Groups, and Average Citizens.*

Noam Chomsky; *Who Rules the World?*

Walter Dean Burnham, Thomas Ferguson; *Why Our Politics Is in Worse Shape Than We Thought,* www.informationclearinghouse. info/article40546

Charles Darwin; *Origin of the Species*

Ibid; *The Descent of Man*

Ibid; *Expression of the Emotions in Man and Animals*

Naomi Klein, *Future Shock*

Alvin and Heidi Tofler, *Revolutionary Wealth*

Ibid, *Future Shock*

Jeremy Rifkin, *The Empathic Civilization*

Sigmund Freud, *The Interpretation of Dreams,*

Ray Kurtzweil, *The Singularity is Near*

www.ingramcontent.com/pod-product-compliance
Lightning Source LLC
Chambersburg PA
CBHW070042210526
45170CB00012B/566